FIVE MARYS WAITING

– A new play by David Banks –

First published in 2012
By PBSK Partnership

Printed and bound in Great Britain by Lightning Source, Milton Keynes

Copyright © 2012 David Banks

All rights reserved.

David Banks is hereby identified as the author of this play in accordance with section 77 of the Copyright, Designs and Patents Act 1988. The author assert his moral rights.

This play is fully protected under the copyright laws of the British Commonwealth of Nations, the United States of America and all countries of the Berne and Universal Copyright Conventions.

All rights including, stage, motion picture, radio, television, public readings, and translations into foreign languages are strictly reserved.

No parts of this publication may lawfully be reproduced in any form or by any means – photocopying, transcript, recording (including video recording), manuscript, electronic, mechanical or otherwise – or be transmitted or stored in a retrieval system, without prior permission.

No characters in this play are based on any real persons living or dead and where similarities may arise with real people they are totally unintentional on the part of the author. Similarly the inclusions of, or references to, any actual institutions, programmes, or named real people, are purely for dramatic effect and are not intended to infer any negative attributes to such organisations or persons, whatsoever.

ISBN 978-0-9574089-1-3

Cover image © 2012 David Banks
Author's photo © 2012 Jane Boyd

FIVE MARYS WAITING

Jerusalem, 44 AD. For eleven years an impassioned Jewish sect has been without its founding leader. His followers, persecuted and scattered, are arguing about his promise to return. Five women meet in an upper room to explore their grief and belief, to remember – and to wait.

DAVID BANKS

For many years, the British actor David Banks has been involved with contemporary writing and original theatre; he is a founder member of the Cherub Theatre Company and the Third I Theatre Company and has been a member of the judging panel for the London Fringe Awards and Artistic Associate with the London New Play Festival.

As an actor, David has played numerous leading roles in regional theatres and the West End. He has had an equally prolific career as a TV actor with, among other appearances, long-running portrayals in Doctor Who, Brookside and Canary Wharf. In addition he has worked extensively as a voice artist in radio, video narration and commercials and has recorded over one hundred talking books including JRR Tolkien's *The Lord of the Rings*.

David's career successfully spans many aspects of theatre and his production of Alan McMurtrie's *The Prisoner's Pumpkin* won Best Play Award when it was first performed at The Old Red Lion, London.

Away from his work in theatre, David is the author of five published books including *Doctor Who – Cybermen* (WH Allen) and the best-selling novel *Iceberg* (Virgin). Other work includes a chamber adaptation of Patrick Hamilton's neglected medieval suspense drama *The Duke in Darkness* (Samuel French).

David's most recently staged play *Severance* tells the story of the medieval lovers Heloise and Abelard.

In one house there will be five divided
– Luke 12:52 –

For myth is at the beginning of literature, and also at its end
– Jorge Luis Borges –

CHARACTERS
MARIA
ROSE
MIRIAM
MADELEINE
SALOME

SCENES
1 Morning
2 Midday
3 Afternoon
4 Evening

An upper room in Jerusalem, Passover, 44 AD.

To Jane
because some myths are true

This play was first presented as a performed reading on 4 November 2012 at The Hostry Festival, Norwich, with the following cast:

MARIA	Anna Patteson
ROSE	Sally Campion-Jones
MIRIAM	Susan Seddon
MADELEINE	Ruth Grey
SALOME	Jen Dewsbury
Director	David Banks

AUTHOR'S PREFACE

Salome is wrong. She and the four other Marys *do* inhabit a play. What they say *is* overheard. The author of their words is in some degree accountable for the words they speak, so here is an attempt to account.

Although there were many early narratives of the life of Jesus, only four gospels were accepted as reliable and canonised by the early Christian Church. Biblical scholars largely agree that Mark is the earliest gospel. They also agree that Mark, Luke and Matthew draw on a body of sayings that is now lost. The discovery of the Gospel of Thomas near Nag Hammadi, Egypt, in 1945 is thought by some to strengthen this view. This Gospel of Thomas is not a narrative but a text composed of 114 sayings, half of which are also found in the canonical gospels.

In writing this play my assumption is that a substantial body of sayings existed in the collective memory of those closest to Jesus, known then as Yeshúa. Men and women were encouraged to memorise scripture from an early age and it would have been natural to commit these sayings to memory in the same way. I also assume that there was a growing call for those sayings to be written down and that this call would be resisted by some. The sayings and scriptures spoken by the Marys in this play are my own adaptations, based on the many translations that exist.

Polonius might call the play comical-tragical-historical. I wanted to write a substantial piece founded in verifiable fact, but with room for creative thought and the mysteries we encounter every day. History is dominated by male actors. Tragedy is populated by fantasy heroes. I set out to create demanding and partly comedic roles solely for female actors across a wide range of ages, characters briefly unburdened (as far as any of us ever can, or want, to be) by parents, children, siblings, spouses, lovers, mentors, subordinates and colleagues. My Marys, for this day at least, gradually find themselves among equals and friends.

How we can exist side by side, despite our differences; love, loss, memory and how the passage of time transforms them; the meaning we ascribe to experience; faith and how it is sustained or lost; the slippery concept of heresy: these are the themes of *Five Marys Waiting*.

My approach is not, in the religious sense, devotional, though I have devoted a year of my life to writing the play, and the ideas it explores have intrigued me since I was a very small child.

If we must trade in the currency of labels the best I can say is that I was once, long ago, a believer and am no longer. The difficulty with labels is that they describe the general and not the particular. A creed is a label. It serves to distinguish, and often to separate, one person from another on the basis of what they profess to believe. A creed is an attempt to ensure that beliefs are identical and, once accepted, never changing.

The early Christian Church would not have survived without some kind of creed to unify it. The difference between 'orthodox' and 'heretical' expressions of faith was hotly disputed from the very start. This should not have been a surprise. Yeshúa of Nazaret was himself executed as a heretical Jew and he had warned his followers that he had come to bring division (Luke 12:51).

Those divisions threatened to become more important than the shared belief. In the very earliest years this must have been bewildering for his followers. How could those who had never known this respected teacher claim a superior understanding of his life and death? Yet they did. Those who had known him must have asked what dispute there could be when it came to faith and belief. Had they not shared the same experiences, known the same man? Yet even they disagreed among each other. They found it difficult and wrong to sign up to someone else's generality of that truth. They each had a particular understanding of the man and the experience. How could this be labelled 'heretical'?

They were suffering an intense sense of loss. At the same time they were being vilified by people who shared their own Jewish faith. The idea that Yeshúa might return to them must have sustained their faith and hope. But the waiting for longed-for deliverance, day after day, year after year, the continued bereavement and persecution, must have brought some of them to the edge of despair.

Salome claims to start the day an optimist and end it a pessimist. One assumes she would find the ending of this play no worse, and certainly no better, than she might have expected. The long wait for confirmation of hope, or despair, continues.

Anyone, now, may turn to Acts 12, and discover what happens after the play ends. If the *Widow's Lament* leads us to expect that 'night is for sorrow and watching for morning', our pessimism will be confounded. That night, we are told, an angel releases Peter from his shackles and leads him out of Herod's prison to freedom. He immediately goes to the house of Mary, mother of John Mark – the Mark who may have written that first reliable gospel – and a very surprised Rhoda eventually answers the door to his persistent knocking.

When this play ends, Salome and the four other Marys do not know what the future holds. They must simply wait. Is it any different for the rest of us? At any time? And isn't it only in the waiting that faith, hope, love, exist?

Laughter and enjoyment in the moment are sometimes regarded as an irrelevance. But they have power to make time stand still, like

> *music heard so deeply*
> *That it is not heard at all, but you are the music*
> *While the music lasts.*

What is TS Eliot describing here in his poem *Four Quartets*? Could it be the kingdom of heaven? No one knows. No one. But there are hints and guesses in the ideas gathered and replicated across many cultures and in our own experience. Hints followed by guesses, as Eliot puts it.

Knock, knock. Who's there? This play is part of my guess.

AUTHOR'S ACKNOWLEDGMENTS

Without the organisers of the Norwich Hostry Festival, and in particular its founder and artistic director Stash Kirkbride, this play would not exist. Rebecca Chapman willed it into being in her quest to discover who the forgotten women of the Bible might be and whether they could make rewarding female performance roles. Friends and strangers, too numerous to mention here, engaged with, discussed and interrogated my ideas for the play and inspired in me the sense that its subject could have an appeal beyond my own personal obsessions.

Rolf de By showered me with authentic bird calls, as well as sound advice, that contributed meaningfully to the play's structure. Connie de Dreu and Robin Forrest gave me confidence in the melodic theme *Waiting* and shed light on its imagined origins. Robin's orchestration evokes the ancient Palestinian setting and transforms despair into joy without changing a note of the original theme. Alan Gold, Robert Wilton and John Yudkin provided invaluable and unlooked-for inspiration. Patricia Papps shared with me her view of angels, which is so deeply embedded in first century Jewish culture. They hover round the edges of the action, messengers incognito.

Sally Campion-Jones, Jen Dewsbury, Ruth Grey, Anna Patteson and Susan Seddon provided their time, enthusiasm and commitment and helped bring the characters laughing and worrying, arguing and singing, into this world.

Jane Boyd believed in the play before it existed and proofread when it was clear that it did. In the space between, she confessed to being a Mary widow, but was nevertheless a true companion on the journey.

The British School at Rome provided accommodation, access to their unique library and a fitting environment to complete the play. My thanks to them and to everyone mentioned above.

Finally, I am grateful to the medical and surgical team at the Ospedale Regionale Oftalmico di Roma, who saved my sight while I was near to completing the play and enabled me to meet my deadline. If Saul of Tarsus had received such swift intervention, how different might Christianity have been?

NOTES ON THE TEXT

Miriam and Salome are from a rural background. Maria and Madeleine are from the city or its suburbs. Rose is a 'foreigner', speaks with a slight accent and lacks absolute fluency in the language spoken by the four other women.

The notes marked by numbers in the text give the documentary and historical references which lie behind the dialogue. In some cases, the characters are intentionally quoting or alluding to these sources. In others, if the references postdate the play, what the characters say is taken to be part of an original source which is now lost, or is assumed to arise from personal knowledge.

Pronunciations: *Salome*, three syllables, with the stress on the first. *Kefa* rhymes with Zephyr. *Ya'akov*, three syllables, stress the first, rhyme the last with cough. *Yeshúa*, three syllables, stress the second, rhyme it with shoe. *Chuza* begins with a glottal h, as in the Scottish loch, which is why Salome can make a joke about it sounding like 'who's a'. *Choni* begins in the same way. *Pesach* is stressed on the first syllable and ends like loch.

A paragraph break within a character's speech indicates a natural pause. Longer pauses are marked in the directions.

The notation | against a speech indicates that it should be spoken at the same time as the similarly marked speech of another character that immediately precedes or follows it.

A plus sign before the part name (e.g. +ROSE) indicates that this actor speaks the lines simultaneously with the actor who is already speaking.

A minus sign indicates that this actor ceases to speak simultaneously with another actor or actors.

MYSTERY PLAY

mysteriously we enter
unknowing, without desire
observing the strange unfolding of the way
secrets moving from shadows into light

at the occasional corner
a glimpse of what might be
the brush of lips, a fragile yearning
wonder, tasting of disbelief

a further turning and the way is clearer
a middle place between desire and possibility
the usual corner to which we keep returning
strong, sustaining, sensible and straight

the way moves on, mysteriously, to where the body is
brings us, unusually, to a narrow darker place
named and unnamed connect and intermingle
white light surges, focusses and heals

extraordinary in every syllable the corner where we find ourselves
transfiguration, death, the holy grail
but where to turn? the white light dazzles
blazing into every corner of the way

soften the glare
move along well-worn paths
meet at unusual corners
observe the strange unfolding of the way

who did it? who's to blame?
no one, it's a mystery
the first and final word
exit now to find ourselves again

mysteriously

David Banks

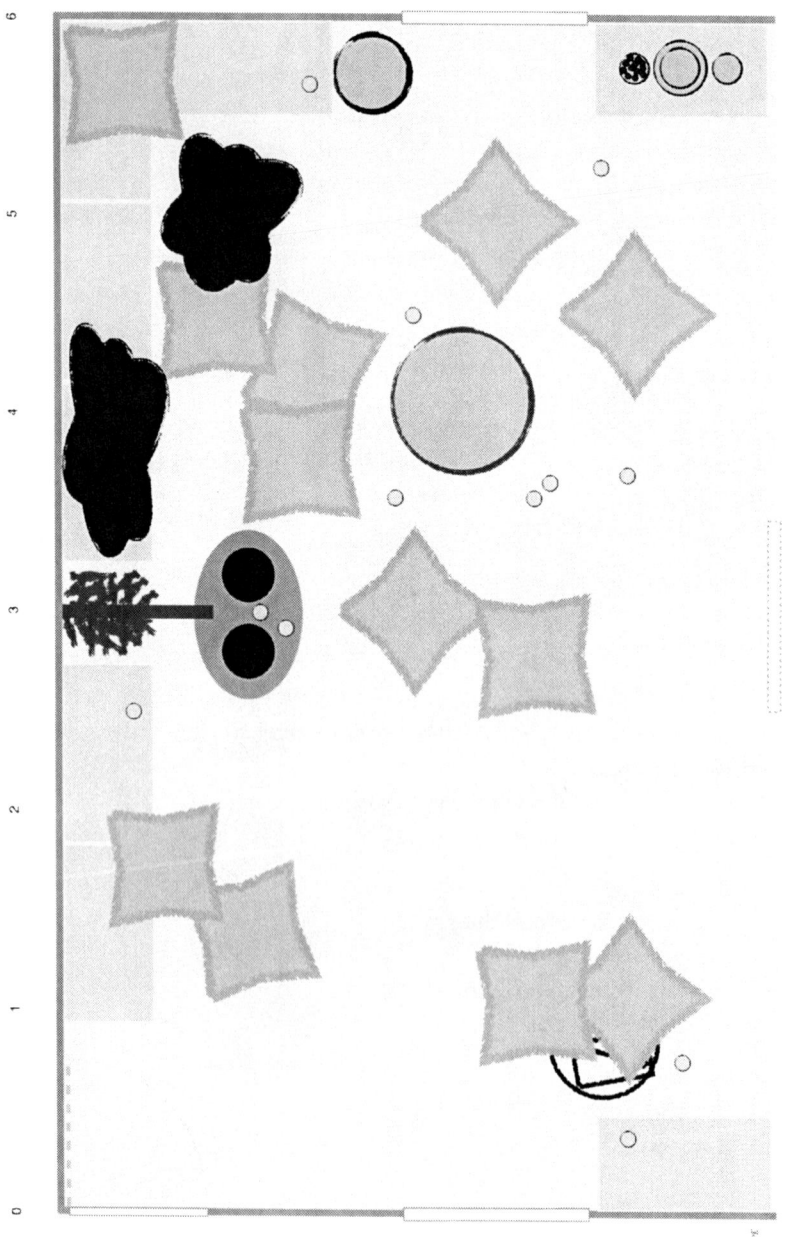

1   MORNING

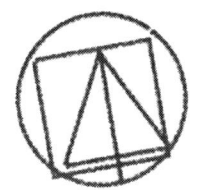

Distant repeated cry of a Stone Curlew.

A spacious room with three large shuttered windows to east, west and south. Next to the west window is a closed door. The back wall is windowless. The south window is to be imagined at the front of the stage. The room is in darkness.

Hoot of a Tawny Owl. Far away, dogs begin to bark.

Dim light of a new day is just perceptible through the shutters of the east facing window. This light will gradually intensify as the scene progresses. Small couches are, for the most part, pushed against the walls. A little way out from the back wall is a wood-burning stove.

Far away an Egyptian and Nubian Nightjar start their repeated call. Much closer, a gentle knocking somewhere outside and a stifled cry.

To the left of the east window stands a large earthenware jar and a jug. To the right of the window, on a wooden platform, is a large bowl containing water. Inside is a smaller bowl, also containing water. To each side is a small bowl. One contains 12 pebbles, the other is empty.

The soft chime of sheep-bells as a flock is led to market. Quietly, a woman's voice sings a slow lament.

Five Marys Waiting: Scene 1 – Morning

Towards the southwest corner of the room, obscured by a cushion, is what looks like graffiti scrawled on the floor in charcoal: a series of roughly drawn geometric shapes.

The room is a complete mess. In the centre, on a low round table, is an enormous round serving plate bearing the remains of food: a few well-gnawed bones and some crusts of bread. Cushions, cups, jugs, smaller plates and more crusts of bread are scattered over the floor. There is a large bundle of black rags on a couch to one side of the stove and nearby a large cloth bag on the floor.

A cock crows twice and the knocking begins again.

Hurried footsteps on stone stairs. The door opens. The silhouette of a woman, perhaps in her mid-forties. She speaks in a loud whisper.

MARIA Rose?

She sighs with exasperation and raises her voice a little.

MARIA Mary Rose?

No answer. She steps away from the door and looks up.

Rhoda? Are you still up there?

A cock crows.

Rhoda? Rose?

ROSE [Off, whispered] Yes, madam.

MARIA Was that you singing?

ROSE [Off] No, madam.

The cock crows again.

2

Five Marys Waiting: Scene 1 – Morning

MARIA	There's someone at the gate. Please see who it is.
ROSE	[Off] I'm sorry, madam, I'm not dressed yet.
MARIA	You overslept?
ROSE	[Off] Yes.
MARIA	You're still in bed?
ROSE	[Off] Yes, madam. Sorry, madam.
MARIA	Then I will go. Rhoda, you are so unreliable.
ROSE	[Off] Yes, madam. Sorry, madam.
MARIA	Have you got oil?
ROSE	[Off] Sorry, madam?
MARIA	In your lamp. Have you plenty of oil?
ROSE	[Off] Yes, madam, I think so.
MARIA	Then light your lamp, throw on some clothes and come down and clean this place.
ROSE	[Off] Yes, madam. Sorry, madam.
MARIA	Remember what I told you. Every crumb. And don't forget to set the clock. It's nearly six.
ROSE	[Off] Yes, madam.

Maria leaves and descends a few steps.

	[Off] Madam?
MARIA	[Off] Shh! Keep your voice down! The men are still asleep, and after last night they have a right to be.
	[Off] Well, what is it?
ROSE	[Off] I can see Mark in the courtyard.

The cock crows again.

Five Marys Waiting: Scene 1 – Morning

	[Off] Could he see who is at the gate?
MARIA	[Off] No, Rhoda. I will go to the gate. If John Mark is awake, he must go to the market. You have the list?
ROSE	[Off] Yes, madam.
MARIA	[Off] Remember, he needs it.

We hear Maria hurry down the steps. Silence. A gentle knocking.

A long way off a flock of chattering Spotted Sandgrouse are approaching in their flight from east to west. There is movement in the bundle of rags, which turns out to be a woman, who might be in her sixties, lying curled in a ball, wearing a black robe and head shawl. She sits up very carefully, covers her face with her hands and remains still for a long moment.

With some difficulty, she gets to her feet, goes to the east window and opens the shutter. She pulls the shawl from her head and stares intently towards the rising sun, watching the approaching birds.

Footsteps on the stairs, descending from above. They halt outside the room, then continue down. The woman turns from the window and listens. More footsteps descend from above. The door opens and a young woman strides in, carrying a dustpan and broom in one hand and a lighted oil lamp in another. She is barely more than twenty. She sees the woman at the window and screams, dropping her dustpan and broom but happily, not the oil lamp. Both women keep their voices deliberately low, so as not to disturb the men.

ROSE	Oh my god! I mean. Hoo! You gave me a fright. Sorry. Sorry. I'm. I didn't know. There was anyone. Here. Forgive me. I'm. Are you, erm?
THE WOMAN	The gardener?
ROSE	Sorry?

Five Marys Waiting: Scene 1 – Morning

THE WOMAN The gardener.

Sudden flutter of wings close by as Spotted Sandgrouse hover over and fly past the house. The woman turns to the window, watching.

Like birds hovering overhead, the Lord Almighty will shield Jerusalem.[1]

ROSE Mariamne Salome?

THE WOMAN Who?

The Lady Mariamne Salome of Cleophas?

THE WOMAN What a title! You must tell her when you meet.

You know of her loss?

ROSE Yes. John Mark said. Will she be here today?

THE WOMAN Yes, I believe she'll be here. I hope that she will. The Lady Salome of Cleophas. She's my sister.

And you are Mary Rose?

ROSE The mistress calls me that. When she's not – erm –

THE WOMAN Angry?

ROSE Mmm. Or – erm –

THE WOMAN In a rush?

Rose stifles a giggle.

I'm sorry, it's –

She sobs.

THE WOMAN I know. I know.

The famine's coming. People despise us. Every knock could be the last. Streets crawling with soldiers. This city is scary for the likes of us. He

Five Marys Waiting: Scene 1 – Morning

will shield us and deliver us. He will 'pass over' and he will rescue us.[2]

Are you new here, Rose?

ROSE   Yes.

THE WOMAN   Antioch?

ROSE   Yes.

THE WOMAN   Rose?

ROSE   Yes.

THE WOMAN   There is something you must know.

ROSE   Yes?

THE WOMAN   You mustn't trust what I say. I often don't know what I'm talking about.

ROSE   Oh.

THE WOMAN   Why are we whispering?

ROSE   The men.

Rose points downwards, then does a mime of sleeping.

THE WOMAN   Ah.

A gate slams in the courtyard.

I'm sorry, madam. The mistress will be back.

She picks up the dustpan and broom, and looks round at the mess.

Oh dear.

She sets down the dustpan and broom and starts to collect the fragments of bread, searching by the light of her lamp. The woman watches for a moment. A Rock Thrush sings out somewhere close, and distantly can be heard the soft chime of sheep-bells. The woman turns to the window again.

Five Marys Waiting: Scene 1 – Morning

THE WOMAN   How everything's changed. New buildings everywhere.

And the birds. So noisy. So busy. As if they have such a lot to do before – what? Before the end? He will 'pass over' and he will rescue us. That's what we are told. That's what this day is for.

Dawn light bursts through the window.

Will it be today? The morning holds such promise. Don't you think, Mary Rose?

ROSE   Promise?

THE WOMAN   Yes, promise. Every morning in these spring days. Such promise. It feels as if anything is possible. Or are we deceived? Is it false dawn? Should we beware? Is it a warning?

Do *you* know what I'm talking about?

ROSE   Sorry?

Rose is busying herself, piling up cushions in her hands.

THE WOMAN   Was it you singing?

ROSE   Sorry?

The woman hugs herself.

Are you cold, madam? I could close the shutter.

THE WOMAN   There are sheep still. Sheep, so close to the city. Wandering under the olives, just as they always have. No sign of the shepherd.

Surprising they haven't all been taken and cooked.

So obedient. So trusting. Fearful too. Fearful of strangers. Perhaps that saves them.

Five Marys Waiting: Scene 1 – Morning

Don't you think?

Rose squints at the light and the woman. Footsteps. She turns. The cushions scatter across the floor. Maria rushes in.

MARIA Rhoda, have you –

Maria sees the woman at the window.

Madeleine? Is that you?

THE WOMAN Have we grown so alike?

MARIA Miriam! The dawn sun was blinding me.

Miriam!

Maria goes to the woman and hugs her, though Miriam continues to hug herself.

James has kept us up with your news.

MIRIAM I've Salome to thank. She kept telling him, keep in touch with your mother – she's a person too.

MARIA Miriam. Her James has been taken.

MIRIAM Yes. For the slaughter.

MARIA You know this?

MIRIAM Madeleine told me. She said Herod's playing politics. The Sanhedrin approved when he arrested James. When he had him beheaded, they liked it even more. And my Jamie's next in line. My little lamb. Shepherd of the flock. It's either him or Kefa. Bound to be.

MARIA Oh, Miriam!

Maria hugs her again.

Five Marys Waiting: Scene 1 – Morning

	Is Madeleine taking care of you? You look exhausted. Have you had anything? We were expecting you early yesterday. Barnabus and Saul set off last night. Back to Antioch. Saul was so sorry not to meet you.
MIRIAM	Was he?
MARIA	Barnabus sent greetings. We were worried. What happened?
MIRIAM	Road block. To be safe we went the valley way and called at Bethany. That's where we heard about James. Poor, poor Salome. She's here?
MARIA	She will be here. She's staying with Philip and Mariamne – and Tau'ma.
MIRIAM	But she hated Tau'ma.
MARIA	No. She didn't hate him. Well, perhaps a little bit, years ago.
MIRIAM	Her jokes incensed him. He didn't hide it.
MARIA	Well, her humour can be something of a strain.
MIRIAM	She questioned everything he said.
MARIA	They didn't quite see eye to eye, that's true. They're very close now. In recent years she's been like a mother.
MIRIAM	To who?
MARIA	To him.

Miriam laughs suddenly.

	Miriam, what is it?
MIRIAM	To who. To him. Salome would say we were a couple of Tawny Owls.

9

Five Marys Waiting: Scene 1 – Morning

MARIA Yes, she might. Though I wouldn't find it funny. Anyway, you mean to whom.

MIRIAM Ah, yes. To whom. To heem. Our Persian friend.

An awkward pause.

MARIA We were talking of Salome, I think. And her loss. And her need. Because John has gone to Cyprus to preach and James has been – well – taken up, Salome needs Tau'ma. She needs him. And he needs her, I think.

MIRIAM How is she?

MARIA She puts on brave face. Keeps us all amused, as she always has. But I'm worried for her. As we were worried for you, Miriam, all those years ago. It takes so long, I know.

MIRIAM What does?

MARIA To forget.

MIRIAM I don't forget.

MARIA Your way of coping isn't mine, I know, so don't take what I say amiss. My late husband was very dear to me. But. Time heals. The pain diminishes with the passing years.

MIRIAM Time is no healer. He was my son. I will never forget. I will never forgive.

MARIA Miriam, remember what he himself said. Forgive us our trespasses. As we forgive –

Miriam puts her fingers in her ears. Maria looks around the room, embarrassed. Absently, she notices the graffiti that is clearly visible now that Rose has removed the cushion that concealed it.

Five Marys Waiting: Scene 1 – Morning

> Rhoda, make sure you get rid of that mark on the floor.

Rose, who has been staring at Miriam all this while, wakes as if from a trance.

ROSE   Sorry, madam?

MARIA   The men have been scrawling with charcoal again. Clean it up.

ROSE   Yes, madam.

MARIA   We were worried for you last night, Miriam, When did you arrive? In the middle of night?

MIRIAM   Just a few hours ago.

MARIA   Who let you in?

MIRIAM   Kefa. He was just leaving.

MARIA   Kefa?

MIRIAM   Yes, Simon Peter. Kefa.

MARIA   I know who Kefa is, Miriam, but where on earth was he going?

MIRIAM   To Joanna, he said. To ask for aid against the famine?

MARIA   Oh. Oh, yes, I see. I see.

MIRIAM   Madeleine offered to go with him. I came up here. Found a warm spot by the stove. Slept.

MARIA   Miriam, we are having to be so careful. Since you left so much has happened.

MIRIAM   I left because so much had happened.

MARIA   Yes, yes, of course. Life is complicated. So complicated. The Lord will provide. But this

Five Marys Waiting: Scene 1 – Morning

	weather. Appalling. The harvests. Terrible. It's the end, I think. It cannot continue. But what to do while we wait? Starve. Cower?
MIRIAM	Pray?
MARIA	Yes, of course, pray. We must always pray. Saul led our prayers last night. He is such a blessing. So intense. So inspired.
MIRIAM	So insufferable.
MARIA	Miriam, he has changed. Beyond recognition. The Lord has wrought wonders.
	But listen, tell me about Galilee. Are things bad there?
MIRIAM	We have fish. We have wells. We have what is needed. I've brought a few things to help fill a gap. And some seeds and a few cuttings.
MARIA	For the garden?
MIRIAM	Yes. I'll plant them and nurture them.
MARIA	We've had precious few rains of blessing this winter.
MIRIAM	The well in the courtyard hasn't run dry, has it?
MARIA	No, thank the Lord. The spring still flows, despite the lack of rain. Rhoda, a cup of water for Miriam.

Rose, goes to the large earthenware jar, pours water from the jug into a cup, filling it to the brim, as Maria speaks.

We have water. Living water.

Rose hands the cup shyly to Miriam and does a little curtsey.

| **ROSE** | My lady. |

MIRIAM Thank you. My cup overflows.

Miriam drinks. There's a flurry of Spanish Sparrows outside the window. Miriam leans out to watch them in the eaves.

Even the sparrow finds a home,
and the swallow a nest for herself,
where she may lay her young.

Maria, blessed are those who dwell in your house.[3]

Maria hugs her again.

MARIA Barnabus and Saul brought supplies from Antioch, but we used up much of their food before they set off again. We still have a little money left. Antioch was very generous. The number of believers there grows day by day. By God's grace. Do you know what name they use for the believers? Oh, they also brought Rhoda, my new serving girl. She's Greek. I call her –

Maria notices the state of the room. As she continues speaking she busies herself, flinging open the shutters of the other two windows and gathering up the large dish and some of the other crockery.

Rhoda, have you done nothing? I know it's chilly outside but we've got to get some fresh air in here. It stinks of stale wine and woodsmoke. The room is in a worse state than when the men left.

Rose has been staring at Miriam again.

ROSE I'm sorry, madam. I was – I was –

MARIA Rhoda, this is your third week with us. You ought to know the routine by now. Barnabus assured me you were reliable. But there's precious little evidence so far. Do you know what the word reliable means? It's a word that is often used in your language. *Axiópistos*? Reliable? Someone who can be trusted?

ROSE   Yes, madam. *Axiópistos.*

MARIA   My question to you is, are you reliable? *Eíste axiópistí?*

ROSE   *Étsi nomízo.* I think so.

MIRIAM   Maria, it's my fault. And this is my bag and belongings. Rhoda wasn't expecting anyone to be here. We got talking.

MARIA   Well, yes, I do understand. She'd have been shocked to see a woman in the upper room. It's usually set aside for the men.

MIRIAM   Even under the new dispensation?

MARIA   I shall have to think about that. Let's talk about this later, when Salome and Madeleine are here. We have the whole day ahead of us. We can prepare everything this morning, have a good chat this afternoon and celebrate Pesach together this evening. Miriam! A feast of remembrance. And we have such a lot to remember.

                 I must get on. The house to clean. Everything to prepare. Rhoda, you were to be up before dawn. Breadcrumbs, breadcrumbs! No need for that lamp now, I can see them clear as day. Sweep them up, every last one. It's what we Jews do. 'And for next seven days you must eat bread without leaven.'[4] Isn't that right, Miriam? Isn't that what the Lord commanded of Moses and Aaron?

Five Marys Waiting: Scene 1 – Morning

MIRIAM	'For on this day in early spring, in the month of Abib, you have been set free.'[5] You get on, Maria. I'll help Rosemary clear this room, before she waits on the men.
MARIA	Rosemary? Oh, yes I see. Mary Rose. Rosemary. Yes. Your heart is always in the garden. Rhoda, pile those plates and cups on this serving dish and I'll take it all downstairs. There's a sink full of washing up to do.
ROSE	Yes, madam.

Rose starts to pile cups and dishes on to the dish.

MARIA	Oh, and Miriam.
MIRIAM	Yes, Maria.
MARIA	There will be no waiting on the men today. They are dedicating Passover to preaching the Word. You will meet them when they wake. They will want to see you and Madeleine before they leave.
MIRIAM	Is Matthew still here?
MARIA	Gone to Phoenicia. He leads the Church there.
MIRIAM	Thaddaeus, Matthias?
MARIA	In Cyprus now. They barely escaped a stoning in the Temple. Had to flee for their lives.
MIRIAM	What about our other Simon? Is he still bright-eyed and zealous?
MARIA	He went to Egypt to evangelise and he's now in Armenia, with Jude.
MIRIAM	Has anyone stayed? Will I see no one?

Five Marys Waiting: Scene 1 – Morning

MARIA There's Andrew. Bartholomew. Peter, when he returns. And most of the women. Susanna. Tabitha. Oh, you haven't met Tabitha, down from Joppa – and that's a wonderful story of God's healing power, another miracle – and then there's Philip's Mariamne and Philip himself of course. But none of them are with us for the feast. They will gather for prayer and Pesach at Philip's tonight. So. No waiting on the men today.

MIRIAM We are set free.

MARIA Miriam, you say the strangest things. But, yes, I suppose. In a way. Yes. Rhoda, chop, chop!

Maria goes to the door, crockery piled high.

Oh, Miriam. We have a new bathroom downstairs, just for the women. A true Mikveh[6]. That spring really is a blessing. Hot water, underfloor heating, steam baths, everything, right up to the minute.

MIRIAM What luxury.

MARIA Chuza's largesse.

MIRIAM Who's Chuza?

She stifles a giggle.

Forgive me, Maria. I'm tired. It just sounds so funny. No really.

She says it more carefully.

Who's Chuza?

MARIA Joanna's husband. Don't you remember? I hope your memory's not going as Salome's seems to be. Chuza looks after us still – secretly of course –

Five Marys Waiting: Scene 1 – Morning

	despite being Herod's Chief Steward. Or maybe because of it. Herods come and Herods seem to go, but Chuza keeps his place, I don't know how. Go down, my dear. Refresh yourself. Rhoda will show you the way. Oh, that reminds me, Rhoda, the boiler needs stoking. And this stove could do with another log or two. These mornings are still chilly. Perhaps we should close the shutters again.
MIRIAM	No leave them. I love the light.
MARIA	You must have been cold in here. And worn out after your journey.
MIRIAM	I am.
MARIA	Go down. Refresh yourself. There are plenty of towels.
MIRIAM	I'll wait till Madeleine arrives. We can explore the facilities together.
MARIA	As you like, my dear. Do you have fresh clothes?
MIRIAM	I'll dig something out of my bag. All my belongings are there.
MARIA	How light you travel. I'd have needed a donkey and an extra mule to carry all my things.

Maria is halfway through the door.

MIRIAM	Maria.
MARIA	My dear?
MIRIAM	Does the Tetrarch Antipas no longer rule?
MARIA	He was exiled. His nephew Agrippa is now the Herod.

Silence.

Five Marys Waiting: Scene 1 – Morning

MIRIAM I've been buried.

MARIA Buried?

MIRIAM In the countryside. Maria, I didn't know. When people said Herod had put James to the sword I imagined it was Herod Antipas.

MARIA Not that it makes any difference. They are all monstrous. The whole tribe.

MIRIAM Worse than our high priests?

MARIA Than the Sanhedrin?

MIRIAM Yes.

MARIA I would say far worse. It's hard to forget what Sanhedrin did, I know. And some are hand in glove with the Roman authorities and with Herod still. Not all of them. High Priest Gamaliel is a good man.

MIRIAM A good Samaritan?

MARIA A good Pharisee. And he supports us.

MIRIAM If this idea or this movement has a human origin, it will collapse. But if it is from God, you will not be able to stop these men.[7]

MARIA Yes. That's what he told them. You will find yourselves fighting God.[8]

MIRIAM Doesn't that sound like fence-sitting to you? They flogged the Twelve, in spite of Gamaliel.

MARIA They are trying to uphold the letter of the law. Our law. Defending the law of Moses.

MIRIAM You mean even if they are murderers and despots, at least they are our murderers and despots?

Five Marys Waiting: Scene 1 – Morning

MARIA   I don't. I don't mean that. I must warn you, Miriam. Be careful. Be careful who hears you say such things. Some take it for heresy.

MIRIAM   Saul, for example?

MARIA   I don't follow.

MIRIAM   Would Saul take it for heresy? The man who persecuted us now preaches the faith he once tried to destroy.[9]

MARIA   Isn't that the most wonderful reversal? He works in such mysterious ways.

MIRIAM   Who, Saul?

                   From the ending of the burnt offerings to the coming of abomination, there will be one thousand two hundred and ninety days.[10] I have counted every one of them. Abomination slouches towards us.

MARIA   I know it's hard to accept the way the Sanhedrin look at these things, the terrible ways they call us to account. But we must bear witness. The flock is growing.

MIRIAM   The flock has run away.

MARIA   You ran away!

A pause. A Woodlark starts its cry. No one moves.

MARIA   I can see breadcrumbs, Rhoda.

ROSE   Yes, madam. Sorry, madam.

Rose starts gathering crumbs.

MARIA   I know why you left us, Miriam. I understand. And, yes, many of the faithful have gone to other cities.

Five Marys Waiting: Scene 1 – Morning

	As it is written, they were scattered. But look what is happening. Word is spreading. The flock *is* growing.
MIRIAM	For it is written. Isn't that what my son told them, the night before they killed him? For it is written. I will strike the shepherd and the sheep of the flock will be scattered.[11]
	Is that why the Sanhedrin struck down my son? To fulfill the scriptures? Is that why the men slunk away? To fulfill the scriptures? Because it is written. Isn't that what he told them? In this very room?
MARIA	Yes, that is what they said.
	Though I believe it was on the Mount of Olives that he spoke those words.
	According to John Mark.

The Woodlark cries again.

MIRIAM	How is your son? I should have asked.
MARIA	He's well.
	He's filled with the spirit. He sets off for Antioch tomorrow. To join Barnabus. And Saul.
	I must get on.
	I'm sorry, my dear. It's difficult. Even after all this time. But our Lord will come back to us. He will. And the suffering will be over. And our tears will be dried.
	Oh, my heart. My heart overflows at the thought.
	I'm so glad to see you again.

20

Five Marys Waiting: Scene 1 – Morning

> Remember to set the clock, Mary Rose. It's coming up to six. Watch the light through the east window.

Maria Leaves. Rose starts to gather up the scattered cushions. Miriam picks one up and throws it hard at the wall in frustrated rage. Rose ducks. Miriam throws another. Rose catches it and arranges it on a couch. A wordless game develops until all the cushions are plumped up and in place and the two women sit comfortably side by side on one of couches.

MIRIAM   Forgive my anger, Rose. An old affliction.

ROSE   You are our Lady Miriam?

MIRIAM   Not lady, no. Miriam will do.

Rose falls to her knees and takes Miriam's hand to kiss it.

> Not that. None of that. Not for me.

ROSE   You are the mother. The mother.

MIRIAM   Yes. Of James. Of little Jamie. Maybe you should direct your reverence to him. He will be next in line.

ROSE   Next to sit at the right hand of God?

MIRIAM   No, that is what Salome wanted for her children. Look where that got them. I ask for nothing. Yet Jamie waits meekly in line for the slaughter.

ROSE   Our lady!

Miriam gently shushes.

> Our Miriam. God works for the good of those who love him.

MIRIAM   Mary Rose. Sweet Mary. Young Rosemary.

> My question to you is, are you reliable?

Five Marys Waiting: Scene 1 – Morning

ROSE — Yes. I think so.

MIRIAM — But are you to be trusted?

ROSE — I don't understand. In my language it is the same. To be reliable and to be trusted.

MIRIAM — Not in ours. Two words. Separate thoughts.

Did you give John Mark the shopping list?

ROSE — Yes.

MIRIAM — When?

ROSE — What?

MIRIAM — When?

When did you have time? You came straight down.

Rose puts her hand to her mouth.

Unless.

If he has the list, you are reliable. But not trustworthy. If he does not have the list, you are not trustworthy and not reliable.

I think he has the list.

It doesn't matter.

ROSE — Our lady.

MIRIAM — Miriam.

ROSE — Miriam. I'd like you to read this.

Rose pulls a small piece of folded parchment from her robe and hands it to Miriam.

MIRIAM — Is it the shopping list?

ROSE — No. It's my reference. From Barnabus.

Five Marys Waiting: Scene 1 – Morning

MIRIAM My eyes are not good. You read it. Can you read?

ROSE Yes! And write! In Greek and Aramaic.

MIRIAM Is this in Aramaic?

ROSE Yes.

MIRIAM Then read.

ROSE 'I commend to you our sister Rhoda, a servant in the church at Antioch, that you may welcome her in the Lord, and help her in whatever she may need from you. For she is young and orphaned and still seeking for the way.'

MIRIAM My poor sweet Rosemary. We must look after you.

ROSE I am reliable.

But perhaps not trustworthy.

Miriam takes Rose's hand between both of hers.

MIRIAM That makes two of us.

A flurry of Spanish Sparrows in the eves. A Laughing Dove makes a loud and repeated cooing. The two women listen for a moment.

ROSE Oh, the clock!

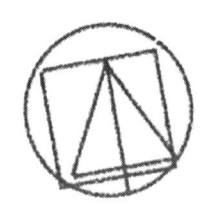

2   MIDDAY

About five hours later. Light no longer pours through the east window but there is bright light outside.

The Laughing Dove is cooing. In the distance is the tinkling of sheep bells gradually moving from east to west. Rose has gone. Miriam is kneeling by the large bowl of water. She is watching it intently, humming to herself the song heard at dawn.

The bowl that had twelve pebbles now contains seven. The bowl that was empty now contains five. Miriam takes a pebble from the fuller bowl of pebbles and turns it thoughtfully in her hand as she watches and hums.

A woman enters through the open door. She is in her late thirties. She takes in the room, goes to the east window and pulls back her headscarf, breathing the air and watching the progress of the sheep. There is an easy intimacy between the two woman. She sings softly a fragment of the song that Miriam is humming.

MADELEINE   '– promise and warning. Midday whispers – '

How green everything is! Flowers and herbs as far as the eye can see. Way up through the olive groves. Everything in bloom. Even without rain. Hard to think it will wither and die in the next few weeks. It all holds such promise.

Five Marys Waiting: Scene 2 – Midday

	But if the rains don't come –
MIRIAM	Madeleine. Look.

Madeleine looks down at the arrangement of bowls.

> This wasn't here five years ago.

They both peer into the bowl for a moment.

MADELEINE	You can see time submerging us.

They watch for another moment.

MIRIAM	There.

Miriam ceremoniously adds the pebble to the bowl with five.

> Twelve. Midday.

Madeleine squints up through the south window.

MADELEINE	Looks about right.

Miriam lifts out the smaller bowl and places it carefully so that it floats on the surface of the water.

	So, the bowl floats on the water and there's a tiny hole in the centre where the water seeps in.
MIRIAM	Like a boat with a leak.
MADELEINE	And those lines circling the inside of the bowl, one circle above the other – each of them shows a tiny part of the hour.
MIRIAM	One part of the hour is already under water. The little boat is sinking already. And when it's entirely scuppered the hour has passed. And I mark it by moving a pebble from this bowl and placing it in

Five Marys Waiting: Scene 2 – Midday

                this bowl. And I salvage the boat and empty it of water and place it again on the still surface. So says Rose.

                And another hour begins. And the bowl that was full becomes empty and the one that was empty becomes full. And the boat slowly sinks all over again.

                It's all so regular. Does time really pass like this? Do our lives really pass like this?

MADELEINE   The days do, so why shouldn't the hours? And the parts of the hours. And the parts of the parts of the hours, like our heartbeats, knocking on the walls of our chests. Knocking without end, until the end.

MIRIAM   The end. Is it today?

MADELEINE   We mustn't expect it. We must always be ready.

MIRIAM   We must always be ready. But how will it happen? I cannot imagine it. I know so little.

Silence.

MADELEINE   Bartholomew's grown into a fine man, don't you think?

MIRIAM   Bartholomew?

MADELEINE   He was always very direct. So direct it could sometimes be hurtful.

MIRIAM   He told me he didn't trust my son at first.

MADELEINE   When did he tell you that?

MIRIAM   Just now. All those years and now he tells me. Is that direct?

MADELEINE   What did you say?

Five Marys Waiting: Scene 2 – Midday

MIRIAM I said I didn't blame him.

Can anything good come out of Nazaret? Do you remember him saying that?

MADELEINE It was before I joined them. They always joked about it. Yeshúa[12] replied, here is a man in whom there is no deception. He sits all day in the shade of a fig tree – and doesn't give a fig about anything.

And now, look at him. No deception. No hurtfulness. Just loving kindness.

MIRIAM He glows.

MADELEINE He does.

Madeleine hums part of the lament.

MIRIAM Another part of the hour gone. Have you seen anything like this thing?

MADELEINE Certain of my clients have them.

They get very tedious. Always have to be watched.

These devices, I mean. Not my clients.

+MIRIAM Necessarily.

They share the joke, affectionately.

MADELEINE Confound the man who first found out
How to distinguish hours!
He hacks our days so wretchedly
And peace of mind devours.[13]

MIRIAM That's not Isaiah.

MADELEINE Plautus. Evidence of a misspent youth.

MIRIAM Pagan.[14]

Five Marys Waiting: Scene 2 – Midday

MADELEINE Him? Or me?

MIRIAM You in your youth. Him? Well, I suppose he lived and died a pagan, so he'll be pagan forever.

MADELEINE He started as a carpenter. Did you know that? Worked with his hands. Then with his mind. A journey some of us have to make.

MIRIAM Some of us.

With me it was the other way round. Now I want nothing more than to work with my hands – making bread, digging weeds, sewing patches. And even this. Being midwife to time. I like it. I can keep my thoughts in their proper place.

MADELEINE Behind locked doors.

MIRIAM Mm-mm.

Under her breath Miriam begins to sing the lament.

'The long afternoon is waiting, waiting.'

MADELEINE When were you different?

MIRIAM Mm?

MADELEINE You say now you work with your hands. When were you different? When did you work with your mind?

MIRIAM When I was young. Way before you knew me. My mind was racing, working away day and night. Worrying, worrying. The whole world was inside my head and I had to control it. Everyone had to fit in.

Poor husband.

Poor children.

Five Marys Waiting: Scene 2 – Midday

Madeleine squeezes Miriam's shoulder.

> You didn't know me then. I had such anger in me. The stories the believers are telling make me out to be some kind of angel. The way Bartholomew was going on about my patience and mildness just now. It isn't true.

MADELEINE This is a man in whom there is no deception.

MIRIAM It isn't true. How would he know? It's a myth.

MADELEINE Some myths can be true.

MIRIAM I don't give a fig. This one isn't. I can hear my heart knocking just thinking about it. Will that make the end come sooner?

MADELEINE The anger I've seen in you I'd call righteous anger. You get impatient at hypocrisy. We both knew someone like that. And we loved him very much.

MIRIAM Yes.

Silence.

> How did you love him?

Silence. Madeleine sees the graffiti.

MADELEINE What's this? A circle. A square. A triangle.

MIRIAM Maria said one of the men had drawn it last night. Using charcoal from the stove. Perhaps he was trying to explain something to the others.

MADELEINE Or perhaps it's the result of a cup of wine too much. Anyway, why does it have to be one of the men?

MIRIAM This is the men's room, apparently.

Five Marys Waiting: Scene 2 – Midday

MADELEINE I thought the men's room was at the rear.

MIRIAM You know what I mean.

MADELEINE Women by appointment only.

MIRIAM Yes, they've gone back to that. Saul's idea. Apparently.

And it was a special evening. The last supper before –

Miriam goes quiet. She is staring at the bowl.

MADELEINE Miriam?

MIRIAM It's all right. Let it be. I thought for a moment my little boat was sinking.

MADELEINE Surely the hour's not gone by already.

MIRIAM Not that. It's Ya'akov's boat. Kefa's boat. Salome's husband's little fishing boat, heaving in the waves. I've put out into deep water and I've let down my nets. Too many fish. Let it be.

She takes in a deep breath and exhales slowly.

Last night was the last supper before Barnabus and Saul went back. Saul was eager to meet us, according to Maria.

MADELEINE Yes, she told me. Several times.

MIRIAM Little Jamie said there had been differences of opinion.

MADELEINE Good to see him after all these months?

MIRIAM Mm-mm. He still looks so young to me. Too young to be helping Kefa lead the church.

Five Marys Waiting: Scene 2 – Midday

MADELEINE We can't keep on calling him Little Jamie. Kefa calls him James the Just.

Silence.

Kefa was telling me about the differences of opinion on the way back here this morning. Only he called them almighty arguments.

MIRIAM Saul has some strange ideas.

MADELEINE Antioch's a young city in a foreign land. It's not surprising that they want to do things differently there.

A triangle. A square. A circle. Perhaps Saul's the artist.

MIRIAM Perhaps. What a thought!

Anyway, Maria called it graffiti and thinks it makes the place look untidy. She told Rosemary to get rid of it.

MADELEINE Rosemary? Oh, you mean –

What's she like? She opened the gate to me when I got back from Joanna's.

MIRIAM Doesn't Kefa have the key?

MADELEINE No one has the key. Everyone must knock. Anyway, Kefa had left the Pesach wine at Joanna's. He had to go back for it. Andrew went with him to keep him company. So I was on my own. I'd been knocking and knocking. The girl seemed very apprehensive. At first I thought she wasn't going to let me in.

MIRIAM She's gatekeeper. One of the many jobs Maria is getting her to do.

Five Marys Waiting: Scene 2 – Midday

> She's right to be wary. It wouldn't be the first time the Sanhedrin has sent a woman to spy out heresy.
>
> Saul wasn't above arranging that sort of trap.

MADELEINE She seems like a little lost lamb.

MIRIAM She is a lost lamb.

> I confused her. I told her I was the gardener. And then I confused myself.

MADELEINE You are a gardener. The land around your hut in Galilee is an oasis. You made it so. And now you're going to make a garden here in the courtyard. You are the gardener.

MIRIAM Yes, but –

> That morning. When we couldn't find him.

MADELEINE Oh. The gardener.

MIRIAM Yes.

Silence.

> What did they do with the body?

Silence.

> Mary Rose.
>
> Her parents died in the earthquake.

MADELEINE Rosemary's parents?

MIRIAM Yes.

MADELEINE How old was she then?

MIRIAM About fourteen.

MADELEINE How did she live?

Five Marys Waiting: Scene 2 – Midday

MIRIAM	By her wits, she said.
MADELEINE	Oh, I know what that means.
MIRIAM	When I look at her, I see myself.
	Before the angel came.
	Madeleine, you're getting me to think. Don't.

Madeleine looks at her pointedly.

	What?
	What?
MADELEINE	Miriam. We've know each other for how long now?
MIRIAM	Eleven years.
MADELEINE	All those years and now you ask me.
MIRIAM	What?
	What?
MADELEINE	How did I love him?
MIRIAM	I wanted to know.
MADELEINE	What?
MIRIAM	How different it was for you.
MADELEINE	And how much the same?
MIRIAM	Yes.
	Because you loved him. So much. I know that.
MADELEINE	Love is too simple a word to have so many meanings.
	The Greeks do it better. They know their loves.
MIRIAM	Madeleine.

Five Marys Waiting: Scene 2 – Midday

MADELEINE   Yes?

MIRIAM   Love is love. Use our language. Just tell me.

Silence.

It doesn't matter.

I know it was different for me. A mother's love is – pulled out of her unbidden. Mothers love because they cannot help themselves, even when their children least deserve it.

MADELEINE   He deserved to be loved.

Miriam picks up a pebble from the bowl and thinks for a moment.

MIRIAM   Yes, he deserved to be loved.

Silence.

MADELEINE   He loved me first. I couldn't help myself. That's all.

Sometimes you discover truth after the event.

Take love as just one example. It starts with an encounter. You have no idea that anything special will happen. But afterwards you realise it has.

From this very personal encounter, you've experienced something universal. A moment in time, a chance event, and something happens that changes your life completely and forever. It becomes the centre of your life. And everything else takes second place.[15]

That's the truth.

Silence.

Why has it taken us so long?

Five Marys Waiting: Scene 2 – Midday

MIRIAM	What?
MADELEINE	To speak of this.
MIRIAM	I couldn't. The time wasn't right.
MADELEINE	And now it is?
MIRIAM	I am here. Back in this room. Somehow time has become a place.
MADELEINE	You are holding the hour in the palm of your hand.
MIRIAM	Yes. With you. Here.

Miriam gently replaces the pebble in the bowl.

>Madeleine. What I'm going to say I would say to no one. No one. And I will not speak of this again.
>
>He was demon-possessed and raving mad.
>
>The clergy were saying it. I thought it too. My son is unhinged. He talked incessantly about his father. As if he knew who his father was.

MADELEINE Oh, but he did.

MIRIAM How could he?

MADELEINE Sovereign Lord, you made heaven and earth and sea and everything in them. You spoke through the mouth of our father. Our father. David. Your child. As with David, so now with us.[16]

>We, the children. The sovereign Lord, our father.

MIRIAM You understood it straight away. I didn't.

>We were just ordinary faithful Jews, leading ordinary faithful lives. Following the laws of Moses, saying our prayers, observing the feasts. Keeping out of the way of the Pharisees. Keeping

our heads down when the Sadducees came to call. Avoiding the soldiers.

But there was one day when he refused to do it anymore.

What you said. Yes. It was true of him. Worked with his hands. Then with his mind. He understood the craft Joseph had shown him. It came naturally. He worked with the grain. Saw under the surface and understood it. He knew where the heart was.

Wood was scarce – and expensive – but the business came pouring in. We had some very rich clients.

Then he began to think.

You say I keep things behind locked doors. You should have seen him. For a long time he said very little at all. Simply worked with the wood.

MADELEINE Teenage boys are like that, aren't they?

MIRIAM Madeleine, he was getting on for thirty! His brothers and sisters had married – apart from Little Jamie. I always thought he'd meet the right woman. Just give it time. I didn't push it.

Salome was always making digs. She wasn't much older. Ya'akov and Yonah were toddlers. I said let it be. But inside I was tied up in knots. Real fishermen's knots.

He seemed so preoccupied. When you asked what he was thinking, the words, the few words he uttered, were very strange. Is it me? he would say. Over and over again. Is it me? Is it me?[17]

Or he would say, Cleave the wood and there am I. Or, Lift up the stone and there you shall find me.[18]

Five Marys Waiting: Scene 2 – Midday

One day he took me aside and asked me, Shall I inherit my father's kingdom?

I didn't know what he meant. I didn't know how to answer him. I was afraid he might be losing his mind.

He'd gone off into the hills when everything was parched, taking no food or water. I didn't see him from one month to the next. He left furniture unfinished. Little Jamie had to placate some very angry customers. I didn't know it at the time but he'd gone off to see Yochanan and his talmidim. They were baptising people. When I saw him next, Yochanan had been arrested by Herod and beheaded and my son was surrounded by talmidim of his own. They weren't much more than teenagers themselves, some of them, were they? And they all looked up to him and blindly did the crazy things he asked of them.

MADELEINE   Not all the time. Not when I was with them. Tau'ma didn't. And Kefa was always trying to prove that he could outrun or out-shout Ya'akov and Yonah. And most of them were forever squabbling about who was the alpha male.

He told them, be wise as serpents and pure as doves.[19] In one ear, out the other. I used to say to him, what are they like? And he said, they're like little children playing in a field. And when the owners come and say, 'This is our field. Scram!', they run away, flinging their clothes off to make good their escape.

Be mindful, he said. Know the world. Anticipate. There must be at least one among you who understands. When the fruit is ripe, it will be

Five Marys Waiting: Scene 2 – Midday

	gathered.[20] They couldn't make head nor tail of it. Only now are they trying to piece it together. The scraps of wisdom.
	He wasn't crazy. He was the sanest man I'd ever met.
	But maybe that's not saying much.
MIRIAM	Ya'akov and Yonah.
	It seems so long ago they were called by those names.
	Ya'akov and Yonah.
	I remember them as children. They were so alive. Eyes like saucers. Into everything. Laughing and crying at the same time. And shouting. Always shouting. Salome had her hands full with those two, the whole time they were growing up. Ya'akov and Yonah. James and John.
	What did he call them when their voices were breaking?
MADELEINE	Boanerges. Sons of thunder.

They laugh.

MIRIAM	Salome loved that joke. What was her reply?
MADELEINE	Ya'akov and Yonah. Boom, boom!

They laugh again.

MIRIAM	How can we laugh when she has just lost Ya'akov? How can we laugh?
MADELEINE	She manages to. As if it's her duty.
MIRIAM	Have you seen her? Is she here?

Five Marys Waiting: Scene 2 – Midday

MADELEINE She was at Johanna's when Kefa and I turned up. She'd already got them to make a donation for Pesach. She went to the market this morning to buy food. She was going to meet John Mark. Maria had drawn up the shopping list.

MIRIAM Ah, yes. I heard about the shopping list.

Distant sounds of Swallows. Madeleine goes to the east window and looks up at the sky.

MADELEINE Have you seen the Swallows? The air is full of them. High up like midges.

MIRIAM They're returning after their winter away[21]. Like us. Returning to the temple. Returning to the fold.

MADELEINE If Swallows can be said to have folds.

MIRIAM If we can be said to be Swallows.

But if Swallows are sheep and sheep are us, then all I can say is –

+MADELEINE It's been a very long winter.

They giggle.

MIRIAM There is something about this day.

Madeleine, do you think –

MADELEINE It's time?

MIRIAM We've waited so long.

Madeleine does not reply but continues to stare at the sky.

Ya'akov and Yonah. Salome was so proud of them. Even when the neighbours told us what my eldest was doing. You could tell they thought he was getting above himself. Preaching in the local

Five Marys Waiting: Scene 2 – Midday

    synagogue. Drawing such crowds. He was just my son, making things up as he always had. Playing the tricks he always had. A few new ones he'd learned from who knows where. Playing a game. A dangerous game.

    But I loved him. What could I do?

    And he talked to the women as if they were –

MADELEINE   What? As if they were human?

MIRIAM   As if they were men.

    No, that doesn't sound right.

MADELEINE   He talked to me as if I was a person, not somebody else's possession.

    That was dangerous too. It was part of the adventure, the excitement.

MIRIAM   Talk to me, men! I'm a person too!

MADELEINE   Yes, he did. And I loved it.

MIRIAM   You loved him.

MADELEINE   He loved me first.

    He pulled the love out of me. Unbidden.

MIRIAM   Did you deserve it?

MADELEINE   He thought I did.

    I didn't know I had it in me. Not that kind of love. I was the one with demons. He seemed to have all the time in the world. Even when Martha came fussing round.

    He looked me in the eye and listened. Nothing seemed to shock him and he seemed to know everything about me.

Five Marys Waiting: Scene 2 – Midday

MIRIAM   As I said. He had a way with wood.

They giggle.

He was good at it, even as a child. The beckoning silence. I'm not sure how he did it but it was very convincing.

MADELEINE   Perhaps because it was true?

He knocked at the door. Martha invited him in. It wasn't the first time I'd seen him. That was months earlier.

Miriam, I can't believe we haven't talked about this before, in all those eleven years! His death brought us together and yet we couldn't speak.

MIRIAM   *I* couldn't speak. I may not be able to speak again.

Just tell me. Just talk to me. Before the waters close. Over my head.

MADELEINE   I was there, down there in the temple. It was in Solomon's Colonnade. Still a building site back then, filled with rubble. Full of bankers. Tables groaning with coins of every type. And the scribes, offering to write the letters that would get other scribes off your back. We were all looking for custom, I suppose. Living by our wits. And it was winter. Snow dusting the ground, and the waiting stones, all carved and waiting to be hauled into place.

And there he was in the middle of it all. Talking about sheep.[22]

She laughs at the memory.

Five Marys Waiting: Scene 2 – Midday

They said he was insane. We are all gods, he said. It's written in the Torah. They picked up stones to hurl at him because what he said was heresy, but he – I don't know, he vanished.

MIRIAM What do you mean, vanished?

MADELEINE He slipped away. Like ice. Like a white cat on snow. One moment, there. The next, gone.

MIRIAM He was always full of tricks.

MADELEINE He was always full of life!

MIRIAM I was so angry with him!

I wonder, sometimes –

Miriam stops short.

MADELEINE Just tell me.

Miriam picks up a pebble from the bowl and thinks for a moment.

MIRIAM I sometimes wonder if that's why things turned out as they did.

The firstborn always get the full strength.

MADELEINE The full strength?

MIRIAM Of our passions. Of our dreams. Of our cruelties.

MADELEINE You were never cruel. I cannot imagine you cruel.

MIRIAM I wish you could persuade me.

MADELEINE I might do. Give me a couple of hours. It's only a pebble or two.

Miriam replaces the pebble in the bowl.

I've just remembered that old proverb.

Five Marys Waiting: Scene 2 – Midday

MIRIAM Go on.

MADELEINE God cannot be everywhere at once. That's why he invented mothers.

MIRIAM Heresy?

MADELEINE No. Hearsay.

Silence, apart from the swarming Swallows.

MADELEINE Rosemary.

I don't have it any more. The oil, I mean.

MIRIAM I have. In there.

Miriam indicates the bag.

MADELEINE Worked a treat for my clients. Soothes the weary limb. Good for embalming too.

Miriam, do you remember –

MIRIAM No.

Enough now. Enough. At least for now.

Madeleine pours a cup of water.

MADELEINE Water?

MIRIAM No.

Madeleine sits on a couch and sips the water. Miriam goes to her bag, gets out a small vial and hands it to Madeleine.

MADELEINE Thanks. I'll make good use of it.

Miriam stands looking out of the south window.

MIRIAM Maria hasn't changed one bit. I thought the years might have softened her.

Five Marys Waiting: Scene 2 – Midday

MADELEINE When I look at her, I see Martha. Not as my sister is now, but when she invited him into the house that first time. Do you mind if I say this? I'll stop if you want.

MIRIAM Go on.

MADELEINE The constant housework. The agitation. She never relaxed. And Maria is the same. Does she ever stop to enjoy anything fully?

MIRIAM She's pious. She's certainly trustworthy. She means so well, but I was arguing with her from the start – when you were with Joanna. I was sleeping just there and having the strangest dream.

MADELEINE What about?

MIRIAM I was being lifted up in a stream of light. And there were two men dressed in white, looking up at me as I rose. I knew them. One was Nicodemus and the other was Joseph.

MADELEINE Your Joseph?

MIRIAM No. Arimathea.[23]

And beneath me, there we all were.

MADELEINE We?

MIRIAM You and Kefa and Joanna and Yonah and Ya'akov and T'auma and all the others. And there I was too. And we were all looking up. At me.

And as I looked down you all became tinier and – at the same time – I was among you and looking up at myself, becoming tinier. And as I was marvelling at how this could be, someone close in my ear whispered, 'Rose! Rose!' I thought it was because they saw me rising into the clouds.

Five Marys Waiting: Scene 2 — Midday

                    Then I realised where I was. I was in this room, waking from the dream, and Maria was calling out for Mary Rose.

                    She was anxious. Harsh. I remembered what the Lord said to Moses. Do not mistreat a foreigner, for you were a foreigner too.[24] And then those other terrible words came crashing in. Consecrate to me all the firstborn. The first offspring to be born, human or animal, belongs to me.[25]

MADELEINE   Not terrible. He was consecrated. Set apart. Anointed.

MIRIAM   They are terrible words. Let it be. Let me ascend into this cloud or it will never pass. Let me simply say how it was. You have always been so good at listening.

MADELEINE   I had the best teacher. I sat at his feet.

MIRIAM   Maria is kind, in her way. But I found myself arguing almost from the start. I am bruised by it all. I need one of your potions.

                    There. I have told you my dream. I have laid bare all my thoughts, on this peculiar day.

                    The cloud has passed.

MADELEINE   I feel sorry for John Mark. No wonder he's leaving for Antioch.

MIRIAM   I think Rosemary –

Footsteps on the stairs. A female voice is heard approaching.

A WOMAN   [Off] Knock, knock.

Madeleine and Miriam exchange a glance.

Five Marys Waiting: Scene 2 – Midday

A WOMAN [Off] Knock, knock.

MADELEINE Who goes there?

A WOMAN No one.

Trying to prompt them.

No one.

MIRIAM No one? Who?

A WOMAN I don't know. I'll go and see.

Footsteps descend. Madeleine and Miriam exchange another glance.

MADELEINE Have you heard what T'auma is doing?

MIRIAM I don't think so. I know he's looking after Salome.

Footsteps on the stairs.

A WOMAN [Off] Knock, knock.

MIRIAM Who goes there?

A WOMAN [Off] No one.

MADELEINE No one who?

A WOMAN [Off] No one I know. Oh bother, I forgot them!

Footsteps descend.

MADELEINE He's writing it all out.

MIRIAM All what?

MADELEINE The scraps of wisdom. The sayings we keep in our heart.

MIRIAM As if my son were a prophet or a king?

MADELEINE As if he were Solomon in all his glory.

Five Marys Waiting: Scene 2 – Midday

Footsteps on the stairs. A woman enters. She is in her early fifties and carries a bag of groceries in each hand. She holds them out in triumph. Despite her words, her manner is clearly depressed.

THE WOMAN Da-dah!

MIRIAM Salome! Salome!

SALOME The shopping! The shopping!

MIRIAM Sis, it's good to see you.

SALOME Do you know what they call us in Antioch?

MADELEINE I've got a feeling you're going to tell us.

SALOME Christians!

　　　　　　I ask you. Christians!

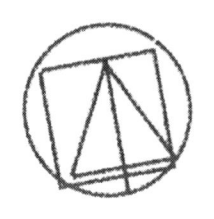

3 AFTERNOON

About an hour later. The sun is spilling into the room through the south window. Outside, there is a gentle knocking.

Salome's bags of shopping have gone. So too have Madeleine and Miriam. Salome is helping Maria to arrange the furniture for the gathering. The couches and cushions are all over the place. When she speaks Salome tends not to move. Maria is moving all the time.

SALOME	I suppose it has a certain ring if you know some Greek.
MARIA	You know some Greek.
SALOME	I know some Greeks. It's not the same thing.

Salome sighs, picks up a jug and brings it to the table.

MARIA	Salome, not there, please. The dish has got to go there. Use your brain.
SALOME	I was using it. To speak. That's obviously the problem. I'll shut up and simply more the furniture.
MARIA	Now I didn't mean it like that, Mary. Please don't take it amiss.
SALOME	Don't you Mary me or I'll Mary you back, Maria. Two can play at that game.

Five Marys Waiting: Scene 3 – Afternoon

Maria is trying to pull a couch into position

MARIA　　Could you just help me with this?

SALOME　　In fact, today, five can play at that game. And probably will before the night's out. Five Marys in a room. I'm sure there's a good joke in there somewhere.

MARIA　　Salome.

SALOME　　Five Marys in a room and four of them Jews. There have got to be jokes.

MARIA　　Salome.

Salome stares out of the south window and sighs.

　　Look at those birds! What on earth do they think they're doing swarming about? Of course, there's nothing on earth about it.

MARIA　　Salome! Can you give me a hand?

SALOME　　Oh, sorry. Where do you want it?

MARIA　　By the table of course.

SALOME　　Yes, but this side or that?

MARIA　　So. That side first. Then we'll put two more there and there.

They move first one couch and then another as Maria talks.

　　I think it's apt. We're undoubtedly followers of the anointed one.

SALOME　　The Messiah.

Five Marys Waiting: Scene 3 – Afternoon

MARIA Yes, but the Greek for Messiah is Khristós. We're followers of Khristós. Iesous Khristós. Jesus the Christ. Do you see?

SALOME But we're simply believers, all of us.

MARIA Just a touch closer. Yes, believers, of course. Believers in the anointed of God.

SALOME But why in Greek? We speak Aramaic. Yeshúa spoke Aramaic. Did he speak Greek? I don't think so. So why in Greek?

MARIA Now that one too.

Because there are probably more believers outside Jerusalem than in it. Because the twelve are apostles and are spreading the message.

SALOME There's another newfangled word. Apostles. What's wrong with the Twelve? That's what he called them. And it makes sense. Twelve tribes of Israel, twelve hours in the day, twelve months in the year. I could go on.

MARIA Please don't.

SALOME So why apostle?

MARIA It means one who is sent away. An emissary.

SALOME I know what it means. I suppose it's Greek?

MARIA Yes, as a matter of fact.

SALOME What did I tell you?

MARIA Salome –

SALOME If they are spreading the message – which I'm all for, by the way – why aren't they called messengers?

Five Marys Waiting: Scene 3 – Afternoon

MARIA	Oh, you mean angels.
SALOME	They're not all angels, I can tell you. I suppose angel is the Greek for messenger?
MARIA	You know it is.
SALOME	I rest my case.
MARIA	Oh dear, this is all wrong.
SALOME	I'm glad you can see it my way.
MARIA	No, I mean all this. The seating arrangements.
SALOME	Maria, today you're catering for five. Tomorrow it's twenty-five. You'll have to shape up.
MARIA	I'm all in a tizz today. Tomorrow can worry about itself.[26]
SALOME	Ah, ha! You see? Don't tell me he didn't tell jokes.
MARIA	Is that one of Yeshúa's? Oh yes, of course. I'm not sure they were jokes, Salome, but even if they were, there's a lot of truth behind them.

Salome sighs.

SALOME	Maria, you haven't answered my question. Why all this Greek?
MARIA	I have, my dear. You just haven't been listening.
SALOME	So what's wrong with Nazarenes?[27] That's what I really want to know.
MARIA	Most of the believers now are Jews who speak Greek. Not Aramaic. Or the old language. But Greek. Take Antioch, for example.
SALOME	Yes, Lord, please take Antioch.

Five Marys Waiting: Scene 3 – Afternoon

MARIA	Do you know it's the third largest city in the world? Greatest number of Greek-speaking Jews. Many have turned to the Lord Jesus Christ, and Saul and Barnabus are winning more every day. Winning them for Christ, who died for our sins, as the scripture foretold.
SALOME	Died for our sins. Is that what they're saying? In Antioch?
MARIA	It's what Saul is preaching. It makes sense of everything. Don't you agree?
SALOME	Maybe if you're in Antioch, it does. But we're Jews, Maria. Why don't we stick to Jewish expressions? All the believers are Jews.

Rose enters, carrying the enormous dish, piled precariously with four bowls and four cups. For lack of hands she carries four napkins in her mouth.

MARIA	That's not true at all. Rhoda, put that straight down on the table and remind me in a minute to check the soup. Have you seen Peter?

Unable to speak, Rose shakes her head.

ROSE	Mm-mm.
SALOME	No she hasn't.
MARIA	Oh dear! He promised to drop by with the Pesach wine.
ROSE	Mm-mm?
SALOME	The what?
MARIA	The wine for Passover. From Joanna's cellar. Well, Herod's really, I suppose. Because her husband's Herod's Chief Steward.

Five Marys Waiting: Scene 3 – Afternoon

SALOME   Who's her husband?

MARIA   Chuza.

SALOME   Yes, who's her husband?

MARIA   Salome, you know perfectly well. Chuza's her husband.

SALOME   Oh, Chuza. Why didn't you say?

So that's why wine wasn't on the list. I was beginning to worry that Saul had banned it.

MARIA   No. A little wine for the stomach's sake.

SALOME   And bring it now for God's sake!

Joke, Maria. Joke.

MARIA   Rhoda, wasn't there somebody knocking just now?

ROSE   Mm?

SALOME   Was there?

MARIA   I'm sure there was somebody knocking at the gate.

ROSE   Mm?

SALOME   When?

MARIA   Just a minute ago. Rhoda, you must have heard it.

ROSE   Mm-mm.

SALOME   No, she didn't. Maria, she was in the bowels of the house, showing Madeleine and Miriam the new facilities.

ROSE   Mm.

SALOME   You see?

Five Marys Waiting: Scene 3 – Afternoon

MARIA Oh, for goodness sake, Rhoda, put the dish down, take the napkins out of your mouth and talk to me like a normal human being.

SALOME Yes, Rhoda, talk to her like a Christian.

As the other two continue talking, Rose carefully negotiates the labyrinth of cushions and couches and sets down the tray, laying out the bowls on the couches, a napkin and cup on each bowl.

MARIA Salome, you're making too much of this. And anyway, it's not true what you said just now.

SALOME What did I say?

MARIA You remember.

SALOME I don't. It goes in one ear and comes out the other. You must know that about me by now. Madeleine tells me it's senile dementia but I don't like to de-mention it.

Rose stifles a laugh. Maria pauses to control her exasperation.

MARIA My dear. You have had a very hard year. And believe me I am very sympathetic. If anything happened to my John Mark, I don't know where I would turn or what I would do, except to lay all my sorrows on Jesus.

SALOME Did you ever meet?

MARIA I'm sorry?

SALOME Did you two ever meet? I'm curious. I hadn't dared de-mention it before, but now is as good a time any. Did you ever talk to Yeshúa?

My nephew?

You know who I'm talking about. Iesous Kristós?

MARIA	Don't provoke me, Salome.
	As it turned out, I never had that privilege. It was my late husband who always made the arrangements.
SALOME	Arrangements?
MARIA	For the use of this upper room. At that time Yeshúa was a – a dangerous man. A dangerous man to know. We had a growing belief in what he was saying and doing. At the same time my husband felt it was safer for us that –
SALOME	Us?
MARIA	John Mark – and me – that it was safer if we weren't directly associated with – well – with what was going on. But we supported him. And we believed in him. And we made it possible for the Twelve to meet in some comfort and privacy.
SALOME	John Mark's a good lad. He's worth his weight in gold.
	I only wondered, Maria. And now I know.
	Believe me, I am very sympathetic.

Salome and Maria hold each others gaze for a moment. Maria starts to move another couch.

MARIA	So. That's out of the way.
SALOME	Looks as though it's very much in the way.
MARIA	No, I don't mean this couch, I mean – well, you know what I mean. Don't provoke me.
	Rhoda, will you help me put this the other side of the table. Then we'll all get a view though a window.

Five Marys Waiting: Scene 3 – Afternoon

SALOME What did you say to Saul when he arrived? And here to the south we have lovely view across the fields towards Bethlehem, birthplace of our dear Lord, and over here to the east the temple and the mount of olives beyond, where he walked and preached, and through this window we come face to face with our nosy neighbours across the street, who make sure they keep up with everything that's new and interesting in the Christian household.

She calls out of the west window.

That's right, madam, a gathering of the innocents! Make sure you let Herod know!

MARIA Shh! Salome! Hold your tongue!

SALOME I can't, the cat's got it.

MARIA You'll get us all into awful trouble.

SALOME There's no one there! Look! No one!

Maria goes to the window and checks.

MARIA Rhoda, help me move this couch.

As they move the couch, Salome notices the graffiti.

SALOME What's this? Is someone designing a floor tile?

MARIA What are you talking about?

SALOME This sketch on the floor. Looks like a fishing boat on a choppy sea. With the sun setting behind it.

MARIA Rhoda, I told you to clean that off the floor.

ROSE Madam, I did, I did.

MARIA Well, you didn't make a very good job of it.

Five Marys Waiting: Scene 3 – Afternoon

ROSE	Someone must have drawn it back again.
MARIA	Is that really likely, Rhoda? If you are going to cover your back with excuses at least have the intelligence to think up something plausible.
SALOME	Cover your back with this graffiti, Rhoda. It would look rather attractive. You may start a fashion.

Footsteps on the stairs.

MADELEINE	[Off] Knock, knock!
SALOME	Who's there?

Madeleine appears at the door with Miriam behind her. They are in a giggly mood.

MADELEINE	No one.
SALOME	No one who?
MADELEINE	No won – der we're on top of the world. We've just climbed all those stairs.
SALOME	You've been working on that one, I can tell. Keep on climbing, you'll get there.

Miriam makes her way through the maze of furniture and sits on a couch near the water clock.

MADELEINE	Looks like there's been an earthquake since we left. Oh, sorry, Rosemary, that was tactless of me.
ROSE	No, no. Thanks for thinking. But I'd be in a sorry state – is that what you say? A sorry state?
MARIA	Yes. A sorry state. A sad state of affairs.
ROSE	So. I'd be in a sad state of affairs if I couldn't bear even to hear that word? I'd need to see a doctor or something.

Five Marys Waiting: Scene 3 – Afternoon

SALOME	Here's a funny one. A certain woman went to the doctor. She had a grape in one ear and a date sticking out of the other, and in each nostril she had a baby carrot. She said, Doctor, I find myself doing the oddest things, can you tell me what's wrong? The doctor took one look at her and said, 'I don't think you're eating properly.' Boom, boom.

Miriam groans, without taking her eyes off the water clock.

	Miriam, what are you up to?
MIRIAM	It's my new occupation. Checking the clock.
SALOME	Well, you're taking your time about it. Boom, boom.
MADELEINE	Oh, Salome, Salome.
SALOME	What? What?
MIRIAM	Come and take a look at this, Sis.
SALOME	Which one of us are you talking to?
MIRIAM	Now who in this room is my sister?
MADELEINE	All of us. We are all your sisters.
MARIA	That's right, we are all sisters in the Lord, including Mary Rose, if only she would invite him in.
SALOME	Oh, is that who was knocking at the gate?
MARIA	Salome don't!
MADELEINE	Rosemary, how would you describe yourself? Are you a believer?
ROSE	I don't really know. Saul and Barnabus have been very kind to me. They took me in to the church when they discovered I was an orphan and the adelphoi welcomed me into their homes.

Five Marys Waiting: Scene 3 – Afternoon

SALOME Adelphoi? That wouldn't happen to be Greek, by any chance?

MADELEINE You know it is, Salome. It means brothers and sisters. The brethren of the church.

SALOME The sistren too.

MADELEINE Yes, the sistren too.

ROSE The adelphoi – you – are like one big family and you all care for each other. It is very – can you say – heartwarming? I am very grateful.

MADELEINE What did your parents believe?

ROSE My parents were sceptics. Followers of a man who died a long time ago. I forget his name.

MADELEINE Followers of Pyrrho?

ROSE Yes, I think so. Pyrrho. I didn't really understand what they meant by being a sceptic.

MADELEINE According to his followers, Pyrrho would have us suspend judgment.

MARIA About what?

MADELEINE About all belief. We should neither affirm a belief as true nor deny a belief as false.

ROSE I remember my parents took nothing for granted. They used to question everything – and I do too. But to be truthful, I really don't know what I believe.

SALOME So your mind is like a rumpled bed.

ROSE How is that?

SALOME Because it's not made up.

ROSE My parents used to say

Five Marys Waiting: Scene 3 – Afternoon

                Those who are intelligent are not dogmatic. Those who are dogmatic are not intelligent.[28]

SALOME   So that was their dogma! How intelligent!

                Sorry, Rose. Don't take what I say in the slightest bit seriously. You must know by now that I'd be the last to throw the first stone. Anyway, I imagine everyone in this room has their bed in some sort of disarray.

MARIA   I really don't think this is the language we should be using as we approach Passover.

SALOME   You mean I should be talking Greek? Or do I speak heresy?

Silence.

MADELEINE   The heresies we should fear are those which are taken for dogma.[29]

SALOME   Now that's a paradox worth thinking about. Is it Greek?

ROSE   When you use this word heresy, it confuses me. In Greek we have a similar word.

MADELEINE   *Aíresis.*

ROSE   Yes, *aíresis*. When *you* use this word it seems to mean *blasphemy*.

MARIA   That's exactly what it is. Taking the Lord's name in vain.

ROSE   But in the language of my parents it means *choosing*. Choosing how to live one's life. Choosing what to believe. Especially for a young person, someone like me who could choose to believe what my parents believed – that we cannot truly believe

Five Marys Waiting: Scene 3 – Afternoon

	anything – if that's what they believed – or in the beauty of Apollo, as some of my friends believed, the beauty of the god of light and the sun, the god of truth and prophecy, or – after the – the –
MADELEINE	Earthquake?
ROSE	Yes, such a difficult word. After the – earthquake – I could choose to believe what those around me believed, those who were spared, those I fell in with. Not very nice some of them. Out for what they could get. Not at all reliable, madam, some of them. But they depended on – superstition, I suppose you would call it – and I fell in with them.
	But now, madam, if I may just say this now, here now. Being here, now, is like starting a new life. A second birth. My gratitude goes out to you for taking me into your house. If I may say some words from your Holy Book of Psalms of David that I have read and stored in my heart?
MARIA	Go on.
ROSE	One day in your courtyard is better than a thousand spent elsewhere. I would rather be a gatekeeper in your house than dwell forever in the tents of the wicked.[30]
MARIA	Mary Rose, I'm touched. And lost for words. Who showed you this scripture? Was it Saul?
ROSE	No, it was Mark. He thought them appropriate.
MARIA	John Mark is steeped in the Psalms. But I wonder he had time to share his learning with you. He's had so much to do before he leaves. Be sure not to get between his legs, won't you, Rhoda?
ROSE	Between his legs?

Five Marys Waiting: Scene 3 – Afternoon

MARIA   Yes, Rhoda. Don't get in his way!

ROSE   Oh yes, madam. I will keep from between his legs.

SALOME   If you talk to her like that you'll have her hankering after the tents of the wicked again.

MARIA   Salome! Witty remarks are all very well when spoken at a proper time. Out of place, they are offensive.[31]

SALOME   I'm honoured you think them witty. But with all this talk of brothers and sisters and adelphoi and sceptics I'll return to my original point if I may. Miriam. Who is your real sister? Who here shares a parent with you?

MIRIAM   No one.

MADELEINE   Where have I heard those words before?

MARIA   Madeleine, please don't start.

MADELEINE   Am I my sister's gatekeeper?

MARIA   You'll only encourage her.

SALOME   No encouragement needed, I assure you. I repeat my question, for the gatekeeper's sake. Who here, Miriam, share's a parent with you?

MIRIAM   No one. You are my sister-in-law.

SALOME   Bull's eye! Yes! You see, I still hadn't succeeded in explaining to good Rhoda here –

MIRIAM   Rosemary –

SALOME   Sorry, Rosemary – how there came to be two Marys in the same family. She must think we're all crazy.

ROSE   No, I don't. Really.

Five Marys Waiting: Scene 3 – Afternoon

SALOME Really, you don't?

ROSE No, I don't.

SALOME You must be crazy not to think us crazy. Our parents called two of their daughters Mary. That's what you think. Isn't it?

ROSE That's what Saul said.

SALOME And then they had to give us other names so we'd know who's who. Is that what he told you?

ROSE Yes.

SALOME The Lady Miriamne Salome of Cleophas! Saul knows our family so well. He's spent all of three weeks in Jerusalem. And then Maria goes and calls you Mary Rose, which is a lovely name, but think about it – because of that, everyone in the room is now called Mary!

MADELEINE Rose, you may think we are named after Moses' sister. But we're not. Our mothers called us Mary after Lady Mariamne.

SALOME It's always the mothers who are to blame. I'll tell you something about mothers. It's atonement day, the most important day in the Holy Temple's calendar, the only day when the high priest can enter the inner sanctum. The new high priest elect is about to be sworn in. And believe it or not, for the very first time in our long, long history, the high priest elect is a woman! The first woman to hold this exalted office – can you believe it? And there she is, about to be anointed before she performs her priestly duties. She's so excited. She stands before a gathering of the highest ranking officials in the Hall of Hewn Stones, right there in the Temple of Jerusalem. Herod's court is represented, the Pharisees and Sadducees are in attendance. And right at the front of the gathering is seated her widowed mother, with the twenty-three judges of the Sanhedrin sitting to either side. On her left hand Herod's steward – Chuza very important man, don't you know – and on her right hand, Herod himself. And just before her daughter stands upon the dais to be sworn in, her mother turns to Herod and says, 'You see that young woman? I'm so proud of her. Her brother's a doctor!'

So, yes, blame the mothers. We're all named after Herod's wife.

ROSE His wife's called Cypros, isn't she?

MARIA It's not this Herod we're talking about, it's not Herod Agrippa. We're talking about his grandfather, the first Herod, who some call Great, though not me. He's the one the Romans decided to call King of the Jews.

ROSE The one who started rebuilding the temple?

MARIA That's right.

ROSE Mark says it's even more splendid than Solomon's temple. Wouldn't you therefore call this Herod great?

MARIA No, I wouldn't. I'd call him a madman who murdered his own family and a great many rabbis.

MIRIAM He was mad with love for Mariamne.

MARIA Or maybe he was just mad. He was evil. Barbaric.

Five Marys Waiting: Scene 3 – Afternoon

MADELEINE These people don't know what they do. They don't know it. Is that evil? Or madness? Or a terrible ignorance?

SALOME It's the same old story. The ruling family and the ruling family's rivals were at each other's throats. But Herod had the big boys behind him, the mighty Roman empire. He was bound to win.

MIRIAM He wanted Mariamne. He was already married with a three year old son, but he wanted Mariamne.

MARIA So he banished them, his wife and his three year old son.

MADELEINE Mariamne was just thirteen years old. Mariamne's mother arranged the betrothal because she hoped to avoid further deaths. It wasn't to be. He loved Mariamne. Passionately. But still he murdered everyone in sight.

MIRIAM One day she despaired. She'd had enough.

MARIA She threw herself from the roof.

MADELEINE Herod kept her body preserved in honey for seven years. Out of love. The kind of madness, or ignorance, that we still call a deed of Herod.

He tried to forget his loss. As Mariamne had thrown herself down from the roof to escape despair, he threw himself upwards, defying the gravity of loss. He flapped his arms and he ordered great buildings to be built – just like Great King Solomon. The great palace and that great temple you see over there and he restored the great walls of the city and built that huge semicircular theatre down there, and then he put up three great towers, the ones you can see right there. And that one, the

	slenderest, the tallest, the mightiest of them all, he named the Mariamne tower. Out of love.
ROSE	What happened then?
MADELEINE	Gravity took over. He plummeted to earth, fell ill in Samaria and died. In Samaria where Mariamne, that thirteen year old girl, had become his wife.

Silence.

SALOME	Now I bet Saul couldn't have told you all that.
MARIA	Shh!
SALOME	What are you shushing me for! I held my tongue for almost all of it.
MARIA	No, listen!
	Rhoda, I'm sure I heard knocking. I think it's Peter at the gate. Go down and let him in, there's an angel.
ROSE	Yes, madam.
MARIA	Oh, and Rose.
ROSE	Yes, madam.
MARIA	Who was it at the gate before?
ROSE	No one.
MARIA	No one?

Maria raises her hand towards Salome to forestall interruption.

ROSE	Yes, madam. Maybe they went away again before I got there.
MARIA	All right. Hurry along then. Chop, chop!
ROSE	Yes, madam.

Five Marys Waiting: Scene 3 – Afternoon

Rose scurries out. Maria struggles with another couch. Madeleine helps her.

MARIA	There, that's just about done it.
MADELEINE	Maria, you go and freshen up now. We're not in a rush. We have the whole afternoon ahead of us.
MARIA	I'm sure I've forgotten something.
MADELEINE	You are worried and upset about many things, Maria, but only one thing matters.[32]
MARIA	I know that very well. Madeleine, you have no idea.
MADELEINE	You think I'm not anxious? We all are.
MARIA	Yes, I'm anxious. I'd just rather you didn't assume what I'm anxious about. Sometimes I find you just a little too patronising.
SALOME	Careful, Maria, if you say harsh things you must expect to hear them in return.
MADELEINE	No, Salome. I spoke out of place. I love Maria like a sister. I love her as my soul, I would protect her as I would protect my very eye.[33]

Silence.

MARIA	I'm sorry, Madeleine. You're right. I am on edge.
MADELEINE	We all are, Maria. No apology needed. My clients sometimes say I patronise. One of my many faults, I know.
MARIA	The Lord will guide. We shall trust in him.
	Now, there are still a few bits and pieces to bring up. You sit down and relax, Madeleine. You are the one who's been up all night. I'm sure there was something I had to – oh, my Lord, the soup!

Five Marys Waiting: Scene 3 – Afternoon

She exits quickly down the stairs. Salome calls after her.

SALOME But Maria, you haven't answered my question. How can you be a Christian if you're not a Jew?[34]

She goes to the door and shouts down the stairs.

> Don't go to the Gentiles or Samaritans, but only to the lost sheep of Israel.[35] Isn't that what he said?

She looks across the street and shouts at an imagined neighbour.

> Just a family quarrel, madam! Nothing to get upset about!

She turns to the other two.

> Some of these neighbours can be very nosy.
>
> But isn't that what he said? Only Israel? Only asking.

MADELEINE I have other sheep, also, which are not of this fold. These I must also bring[36]

SALOME Really? Did he say that? How big did he say his father's house was?

MIRIAM Come and sit by me and take a look at this, Sis.

SALOME If you insis, Sis.

Salome sits next to Miriam, who gently grasps Salome's hand. Madeleine stands behind them both, laying a hand on each.

MIRIAM Let's just watch and wait.

SALOME What are we waiting for?

MIRIAM It's coming up to three.

68

Five Marys Waiting: Scene 3 – Afternoon

SALOME How can you tell from that? Looks like the washing up.

MADELEINE So. The bowl floats on the water and there's a tiny hole in the centre where the water seeps in –

SALOME No, don't tell me. I'm incredibly impatient with new technology. Let it remain a mystery.

MIRIAM Watch. Wait.

MADELEINE There's a lot to be said for mystery.

Quietly, calmly, Madeleine begins to pray. First Miriam and then Salome join in.

MADELEINE Praise the Lord, you his servants,
both now and forevermore.

+MIRIAM From the rising of the sun
to the place where it sets,
He stoops down to look
on the heavens and the earth.

+SALOME He raises the poor from the dust
and lifts the needy from the ash heap.
He seats them with princes.[37]

There is a moment of utter peace and silence before the distant tinkling of sheep bells is heard.

SALOME What a sunrise this morning! It just filled me with hope. That's my trouble. I wake up an optimist and go to bed a pessimist.

She sighs. Miriam picks up a pebble from the bowl with five in it.

MIRIAM There.

She places the pebble in the bowl that contains seven.

Five Marys Waiting: Scene 3 – Afternoon

Two in the afternoon.

Salome squints up through the south window.

SALOME Looks about right.

Unnoticed, Rose has appeared and watches from the door.

Miriam lifts out the smaller bowl from the large bowl of water and places it carefully so that it floats on the surface.

MIRIAM When we came out of Egypt
the sea looked and fled,
the mountains leaped like lambs.

SALOME Why was it, sea, that you fled?
Why, mountains, did you leap like lambs?

MADELEINE Tremble at the presence of the Lord.
He turns the rock into a pool,
Flint into living water.[38]

Silence, except for the distant tinkling of sheep bells. Miriam gets up to go to her bag and sees Rhoda.

MIRIAM Rosemary, come and join us. Was it Kefa?

ROSE I don't know, Miriam. The mistress said she would go and see and told me to come back here and wait on you. The three Marys.

MADELEINE Let's wait on each other. I hope you'll stay and talk to us this afternoon, Rosemary. I'm longing to hear about Antioch. I see you've only set four places. You will join us, won't you?

ROSE The mistress has given me tasks to do.

MADELEINE If I know Maria she's preparing for doomsday. I'm sure they can wait.

Five Marys Waiting: Scene 3 – Afternoon

SALOME Or if not, we can all set to and do them, can't we Marys?

MADELEINE I'll have a word with her and set a place for you myself. But tell us a bit about Antioch. I've never been. What's it like?

ROSE Big. A big city. Much bigger than this one. Much of it ruined now, since the – the –

SALOME Earthquake?

ROSE Yes. Earthquake. Such a difficult word.

When I was growing up it had these huge marble colonnades, four times the size of the one in your temple over there. The Romans had built wide paved streets, going straight from one end of the city to the other, and we had beautiful bathing pools that everybody swam in every day, and open-air theatres with actors in masks and on stilts and big booming voices and – what else?

Yes, markets. The markets. Filled with every food you could think of. And squares and piazzas and the street lamps at night. And magical statues of Apollo, naked and beautiful and true, true to life. You could stand there and imagine him stepping down and taking you by the hand. And there was Zeus with his daughter Selene, the goddess of the moon with her radiant immortal head and golden crown.

That's what I remember of it when I was young. One day all of that was there – a paradise. The next it was gone. Because of the –

Earthquake.

Five Marys Waiting: Scene 3 — *Afternoon*

Silence. Miriam has taken a small wooden box out of her bag. She hands it to Rose.

MIRIAM Rosemary. Rose. You see this box? Look inside. What do you see?

ROSE A brown ball. A tangle of hemp string?

MIRIAM It's a plant. It's dead. Many years ago I picked the flowers from the sea shore near our home. I kept them alive for a long time. They meant a lot to me. But one day they died. Quite suddenly.

ROSE What is it called?

MIRIAM Rose. The Rose of Jericho.

I've heard it would come back to life if the conditions were right. Apparently, it's like a miracle.

So I carefully placed the dead plant in this little box, waiting for a special day. For resurrection.

I think the day is here. Will you perform a miracle?

ROSE Gladly. What shall I do?

MIRIAM Put an empty bowl close by the window. So it stays in the sun.

Rose takes a bowl from the table a places it on the floor in the sun.

Pour a little water in it.

Rose takes the water jug and half fills the bowl.

Now take out the dead plant – gently – and place it in the bowl.

Rose does this.

72

Five Marys Waiting: Scene 3 – Afternoon

	What do you see?
ROSE	Nothing. The fibres are going dark. Soaking up the water.
MIRIAM	We'll have to wait. Let's forget about it now. Miracles must always take you by surprise.
SALOME	Some rain now would take us by surprise. Even Rabbi Choni couldn't bring life to the Rose of Jericho.
ROSE	I know so little about these things. Rabbi Choni?
MADELEINE	Rabbi Choni brought the rains.
SALOME	That's one thing Yeshúa never did.
MIRIAM	Rabbi Choni. The circle drawer. You bring him back to me. Anna was his talmid when she was young.
ROSE	Anna? Talmid? I'm lost.
MADELEINE	Talmid is disciple. Anna was a prophet in the temple.
MIRIAM	She was such a great age. I always took the time to speak to her whenever I visited the temple. She had lived there since her husband had died – eighty years before. So she said.
ROSE	But that would have made her – let me see –
SALOME	A hundred and three!
MIRIAM	Perhaps she was. Who knows.
SALOME	No one!
MIRIAM	So. She blessed my firstborn. She blessed him and called him a king. She spoke of the redemption of Jerusalem.[39] This disciple of Rabbi Choni.

ROSE	And she was a drawer of circles?
MADELEINE	Rabbi Choni was the drawer of circles. He lived and died a hundred years ago. The story of the rain is this. There had been none for a whole season.
SALOME	Sounds familiar.
MADELEINE	The wells were dry and the plants were withering in the ground. So they asked Rabbi Choni to pray for rain to fall. He answered, 'Bring in the Pesach ovens, so that they may not be softened by the rain.' They were made of mud, you see.
	He prayed, and he prayed, but the rain did not fall. So what did he do? He drew a circle on the ground.
ROSE	As in this graffiti.
MADELEINE	Exactly. He drew a circle on the ground but it was big enough for him to stand within it. And he stood within it. And he raised his hands in prayer and he said, 'O Lord of the heavens, your children have turned their faces to me, because I am like the eldest son before you. I swear by your great name that I will not move from here until you show mercy upon your children.'
	And on his cheek he felt a drop of rain, and then another, and then nothing more. He said, 'Not for such rain have I prayed, but for rain that will fill the wells and the caverns.' And indeed it began to rain a little more, a fine drizzle that wet his cheeks but was lost the minute it touched the parched earth. So raising his hands again he cried, 'Not for such rain have I prayed, O Lord, but for rain of blessing and abundant grace.' Then the rains came down in torrents and the wells and the caverns were filled, and still it continued. And the rivers overran their

	banks. And the people went up to Jerusalem to the Temple Mount because of the rain. And they sought out Rabbi Choni. And they begged him, they begged him, 'As you prayed for rains to come down – please now –
+MARIA	'Pray it may go away!'
SALOME	And the moral of the story is?
ROSE	Be careful what you ask for. Be wary of the power of circles.

Silence. The other women look at her curiously.

	Another thing I don't understand. The Samaritans.
SALOME	Who does?
ROSE	But aren't the Samaritans descended from Abraham just like you? Why do the Jews think of them as the enemy?
MIRIAM	It's a very long story.
SALOME	We'll put it in context for you. Who do you think of as the lowest of the low?
ROSE	I don't like bankers very much. You know, the money changers.
MADELEINE	He would have agreed with you. When he found them in the temple he got a whip and threw them out and overturned their tables.
ROSE	Was he an angry man?
SALOME	He was that day. What a sight! It didn't endear him to the authorities, I can tell you. He said it's easier for a rich man to go through the eye of a needle[40] –
MADELEINE	Elephant.

Five Marys Waiting: Scene 3 – Afternoon

SALOME	Elephant? How could an elephant go through the eye of a needle?
ROSE	How could a rich man? How could any of us?
MIRIAM	Isn't that the point?
SALOME	Sorry, we're losing the plot. If this were a play the audience would think we'd mixed up our lines.
MIRIAM	I know this. A needle's eye is not too narrow for two friends, but the world is not wide enough for two enemies.[41]
SALOME	Ah, yes. Enemies. So have you heard the one he might have told? About the priest, the charity-worker and the banker? They all went down from Jerusalem to Jericho – down that road you can see just there –

She points out of the east window at a point in the middle distance.

– though of course not together. That would never do.

The priest was the early bird. He set off before it was light and he came to a deserted stretch and saw something lying in the ditch – a man, beaten by robbers, stripped of his clothes, bleeding, half-dead. The priest backed away and scuttled off down the road to get to Jericho in time for an important service. As the sun rose little higher in the sky, the charity-worker came along and she saw the man lying in the ditch and she backed away and scuttled off down the road to get to Jericho in time for a vital fundraising meeting. By the time banker came along, the sun was high and the man was covered in flies and, quite frankly, beginning to smell. And the banker was leading a donkey, which was loaded with supplies from his business trip in Jerusalem. And he had to travel well beyond Jericho. And he was so looking forward to getting home and greeting his wife and having a slap up meal.

But as soon as he saw how badly the man was injured, he ran and tended to his wounds, brought him to an inn and paid out two days wages – a huge amount of money – to make sure he was well looked after. And if you need any more, he said –

+MIRIAM Just let me know!

ROSE That doesn't sound like a banker to me.

MADELEINE He showed compassion. The others hurried on. Do we get grapes from a thorn bush or figs from a thistle? We show what we are by the deeds that we do.[42]

ROSE So. With enemies like that banker, who needs friends?

SALOME Too late, you've got some now.

ROSE Enemies?

SALOME No, friends.

MADELEINE I'll go down and get two extra bowls, one of them for Rose. Then you can tell us more about Antioch.

As she heads for the door Maria rushes in, carrying a jug.

MARIA Madeleine, take this! I must close this shutter, quick. Block out the street.

She thrusts the jug into Madeleine's hands and closes the shutter of the west window.

Five Marys Waiting: Scene 3 – Afternoon

MADELEINE Maria, what's happened?

MARIA It's Kefa.

They've arrested him.

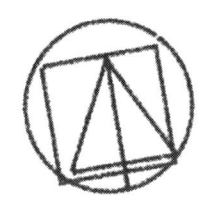

4 EVENING

About three hours later. There is intense light around the edges of the shuttered west window. Maria is sitting at the table, her voice rushed and weak, her arms lifted in prayer. Sitting on either side, Salome and Rose support her arms. Miriam sits watching the clock. Madeleine peers out of the east window.

MARIA Sovereign Lord, you made heaven and earth and sea and everything in them. Thus you spoke through the mouth of our father David. 'Why do nations rage and peoples plot in vain and kings and rulers conspire against the Lord and his Anointed One?' As with David, so now with us. Herod and Pontius Pilate and the Gentiles and the people of Israel. They do what your power decrees they must. Now, Lord, consider their threats. Enable your servants to speak your word with boldness. Stretch out your hand to heal with signs and wonders.[43]

Amen.

ALL Amen.

MARIA Sovereign Lord –

She falters and swallows hard.

Five Marys Waiting: Scene 4 – Evening

SALOME Rest, Maria, rest. You've been praying for hours. Let one of us lead.

Maria nods and lowers her arms. Rose hands her a cup.

ROSE Madam? Water?

MARIA Thank you. Yes.

Maria slowly drains the cup and sets it down.

I shall raise the cup of salvation, and call upon the name of the Lord.[44]

SALOME You've already done that, Maria. You've called on him so often, the ears of the Lord will be hurting.

His will be done. Enough now. Enough.

Silence.

MADELEINE I think I see something.

No, wait.

False alarm.

What is the time, Miriam?

MIRIAM Sinking down to six.

ROSE Looks about right.

SALOME Pesach approacheth. Surely I can go down and get the food.

MARIA No! We mustn't leave this room. Andrew said we mustn't leave this room. The soldiers might see us and raise the alarm.

MADELEINE So you say. And he may be right. But remember he got a terrible fright himself. He might be overreacting.

Five Marys Waiting: Scene 4 – Evening

Silence.

SALOME What do we have here? To mark Passover?

MIRIAM I've some loaves in my bag. And some dried fish.

SALOME That's a start.

Miriam goes to her bag and hands them to Rose who, with the help of the other women, sets out the items on the serving dish.

MIRIAM Olive oil. Precious salt. Matzo – Rose, this matzo is our soft unleavened bread. Five little loaves of it. Two fish.

SALOME Enough for a feast.

MIRIAM Olives. Nuts. Dried figs. Dried apricots. A few sticks of celery.

MADELEINE The celery will do for the karpas.

ROSE What is the karpas?

MARIA It's one of our Passover rituals. We dip a vegetable in salty water and eat it. The salt water is for the tears we shed when we were slaves in Egypt.

ROSE How long ago was that?

MARIA To be honest, I don't exactly know. A thousand years?

SALOME At least.

ROSE So long. And you still remember?

MIRIAM We carry the past wherever we go.

MARIA It's been a long, long journey. Salt tears all the way.

SALOME You know the riddle? The more you take the more you leave behind.

Five Marys Waiting: Scene 4 — Evening

ROSE	Memories?
SALOME	No. Footsteps. The more you take the more you leave behind.
MIRIAM	Memories you never leave behind.
ROSE	No. That's true.

Silence.

MADELEINE	What about the wine?
MARIA	It's in the jug.

Madeleine picks up the jug that Maria brought in and sniffs at it.

MADELEINE	It's good. This is what Andrew brought?
MARIA	He and Peter were on their way back with it.
MIRIAM	You say Herod's guards appeared out of nowhere?
MARIA	Those were his words. He said they dragged Kefa away and left Andrew standing in the road with the wine. He came here immediately. Stay in the upper room, he said. Close the shutters looking on to the street. Pray. Pray for Peter's release.
MIRIAM	We've done that unceasingly.
SALOME	We did it for Ya'akov.
MARIA	Then Andrew went down to join the others. They'd signal when it was safe to come out. He said to keep watch on Philip's house.
MADELEINE	Which we've been doing. Unceasingly.

Rose joins Madeleine at the east window.

ROSE	Which is Philip's house?

MADELEINE	Below the west wall of the temple. You see the big circular roof of Herod's theatre?
ROSE	Yes.
MADELEINE	Down below that, in the lower city, to the right. The flat red roof? Two palm trees on it?
ROSE	I see it. So how would they signal? Flashing a mirror?
MADELEINE	Yes. That's what I thought I saw just now. But the flashing would have continued until we responded in kind. If it's night they light a brazier and use sulphur to make it flash.
MARIA	Rhoda, if we get a signal you must go up at once and return it until they stop signalling.
ROSE	Yes, madam.
MADELEINE	We can wait, but we don't need to watch all the time. The light will flash into the room. And while we wait we must celebrate Pesach.
SALOME	How would they know it was safe? It's never safe. Will Herod's guards go to Philip and say, sorry, Guv, our mistake? We forgot it was Passover.
MIRIAM	They might release him, after a night in prison.
SALOME	Talk sense, Miriam. Did they spare Stephen? Did they release my James?
MADELEINE	James was our leader, our shepherd.
SALOME	So is Peter.
MADELEINE	Yes, that's my point. And so, now, is Miriam's James. They are all tokens in a game Herod is playing with the Sanhedrin. Your James was first. Peter may be next.

Five Marys Waiting: Scene 4 – Evening

MARIA	No!
MIRIAM	It's true. He may be. And then my James.
MADELEINE	We must face this steadily. We must each have the courage that Salome and Miriam have shown.
	Strike the shepherd and scatter the sheep. He's playing politics. Again. And the High Priests are lapping it up.
SALOME	Yeshúa called them dogs. He was right.
ROSE	Dogs?
SALOME	Yes, dogs in a manger. The Scribes, the Pharisees, the Sadducees – the whole misguided clergy. They lie around like dogs in a manger, not eating the food that's meant for the cattle – and not letting the cattle eat it either! Let them rot, he said, the whole damn lot of them.[45]
MARIA	I'm sure he didn't say anything of the sort.
SALOME	Madeleine, you knew him. Am I right? Or am I right?
MADELEINE	May misery come upon the clergy. They are whitewashed tombs hiding dead men's bones,[46] the blind leading the blind.[47]
SALOME	Why do you think they wanted him dead? You said yourself – when you were moving the furniture – he was a bit too dangerous to know.
MADELEINE	Don't think I have come to cast peace upon the world. I bring division. Fire, sword, war.[48]
MARIA	I can't believe he said that. From what I've heard he was kind, he was loving.

84

Five Marys Waiting: Scene 4 – Evening

MADELEINE   He was a thorn in the flesh! Rebellious, provocative, cunning, alive! He knew the world. He dared it to know him. Be wise as vipers, as well as pure as doves.

The world is not easy. The truth is more complicated than you think. Begin to speak it and you will have committed heresy.

He said: I shall give to you what eye has not seen and what ear has not heard.[49] He knew what would come. To him and to us. Fire, sword, war. Unavoidable.

Listen. He said: Five shall be in a house – three against two and two against three, sister against sister. And they shall all be together. And they shall all be alone.

With a despairing sigh Miriam slumps down on a couch.

SALOME   Don't sigh, Sis. That's my job.

MIRIAM   I thought there would be an end to it. It doesn't end. I was hoping for a miracle. I was hoping this was the day.

And look. My Rose of Jericho. It hasn't bloomed.

ROSE   Maybe it needs just another day of sunlight.

Silence.

MARIA   People give such different accounts. Saul did not meet him in the flesh, but he has in the spirit and during these last weeks here he has given us such wonderful assurance and guidance about how to be a Christian. How can we rely on your account, Madeleine?

Five Marys Waiting: Scene 4 – Evening

MADELEINE I cannot say, Maria. I cannot give you that assurance. It is for each of us to know what we can believe.

I can say this. I was there. I was with him. He talked to me. I talked to him.

MARIA What about writing it down? Saul writes such glorious, uplifting letters. Encourage the timid. Care for the weak. Be patient with everyone. Don't pay back evil for evil, but always strive to do good.[50] Wonderful words. Wonderful sentiments. All written down.

MADELEINE Platitudes. A sheep bleating to the sheep.

Silence.

MARIA I'm afraid I don't agree.

If only some of Yeshúa's words were written down.

SALOME We're doing just that, Maria. I'm helping Tau'ma to do exactly that.

MARIA Yes, I know. I look forward to studying them.

MADELEINE I'm sorry, Salome, it will not do.

Scraps dropped from the table after the sumptuous meal has been cleared away. The remnants of a feast that only those present could ever enjoy to the full.

SALOME Madeleine. I don't despair easily, as you know. But you are bringing me close to the edge. And if to despair is a sin, remember he also said something like this. If anyone causes one of these little ones to sin, it would be better for him to be thrown into the sea. With a large millstone tied around his neck.

Five Marys Waiting: Scene 4 – Evening

MARIA   This is just awful. I cannot believe he said these things.

MADELEINE   Salome, forgive me. Forgive me, all of you. The time carries me away. I would have none of you despair. I mean only to say this.

Those of us who knew him, know his words. Their meaning is impressed on our hearts.

Whoever, as time goes on, writes accounts of his life will give their own view of it. The truth will be obscured, or lost, or scattered like seed on the wind.

MARIA   You give your own account of it.

MADELEINE   You know me.

I knew him.

You take me on trust or you don't.

You believe me or you don't.

Can you rely on me? That's for you to say. It's not enough that I appear reliable. In the end you have to know that you trust me.[51]

Rose goes to the clock and picks up the last pebble from the almost empty bowl and waits a moment. The others watch her.

ROSE   There. Six.

One bowl is empty. The other is full.

She places the pebble in the other bowl, lifts out the smaller bowl from the large bowl of water and places it carefully so that it floats on the surface.

MADELEINE   The time carries us away. Rose, you'll join us for Pesach?

Five Marys Waiting: Scene 4 – Evening

ROSE If my mistress will allow me.

MARIA Gladly. Here's a cup. But we need two bowls.

ROSE We do, don't we.

She empties the bowl of pebbles and picks up both empty bowls.

Will these do?

Apart from Maria, the other women react with delight.

MARIA But what about the time?

MADELEINE Time was made to serve us, not us to serve time.

SALOME As Yeshúa said of the Sabbath.

MARIA I'm sure he didn't.

SALOME We'll ask him when he comes. Sit round, sisters.

The distant tinkling of sheep bells gradually moving from east to west can occasionally be heard. Miriam goes to look out of the south window as the others arrange themselves round the table and distribute the food.

Break the bread. Pour the wine. Let's eat.

MARIA And remember!

SALOME I have an overwhelming urge to strangle any person who suggests I should start wallowing in the past.[52]

Joke, Maria. It's a joke. Plautus, I think.

It's true. There's a place for memory. If only I knew where I put mine.

Madeleine pours the wine.

MADELEINE Maria, your cup.

Five Marys Waiting: Scene 4 – Evening

MARIA Thank you, Madeleine.

MADELEINE Salome. Tell me when.

SALOME I'll go by the clock.

MADELEINE Sweet Rosemary, will you partake?

ROSE Indeed, my lady. For my good health's sake.

MADELEINE And the first shall be last. Miriam?

Miriam?

MIRIAM Oh, sorry. I was away in the fields. I stopped to think and forgot to start again.[53]

MADELEINE A cup of wine for Pesach?

MIRIAM Just water for me.

ROSE I'll get it.

She fetches the water jug and fills Miriam's cup as Madeleine fills her own.

MIRIAM I'm watching the sheep. Thinking of the shepherd – another of our shepherds – taken away from us.

I'm wondering if despair is sin, and hoping desperately it isn't.

I'm thinking about trust and know it's misplaced in me.

You all took me in, took me into your homes, as you have taken sweet Rosemary in. You shared what you had, you cared for me as your very soul.

You mourned my son, you promised he would return.

He never did. I never saw him again. Not even his body.

Five Marys Waiting: Scene 4 – Evening

> So I left you all and went back to my hut in Galilee. I despaired. The millstone was around my neck. But there was no roof high enough to escape my despair.
>
> So I stepped on a snake.
>
> A deadly black snake.
>
> I wanted the serpent to take my life away.

Silence.

ROSE   My lady! What happened?

Silence.

MIRIAM   It died.

She stifles a giggle.

> I'm sorry, it's –

She sobs.

ROSE   I know. I know.

MADELEINE   She shall crush his head.[54]

Silence.

MIRIAM   So. I'm watching the sheep. Thinking of the shepherd.

> The Lord is my shepherd.
> We have all that we need.

+MADELEINE   He lets us lie down in green pastures.
He leads us beside restful waters.
He restores our soul.

Five Marys Waiting: Scene 4 — Evening

+SALOME	He guides us home. In this valley of death, we will not fear evil.
+MARIA	For you are with us. Your shepherd's staff consoles us.
−MARIA	You provide us with food in the midst of famine. You anoint our head with oil. Our cup overflows.
−MADELEINE	Your goodness and steadfast love shall be with us all the days of our life,
−SALOME	and we shall dwell within your house for ever.[55]

Rose hands Miriam the water.

ROSE	A cup for Miriam.
MIRIAM	Thank you, Mary Rose.
MADELEINE	Five Marys in a room And four of them were Jews. Who could be the odd one out? Who would Jesus choose?

Silence.

SALOME	Drink, Marys. To the shepherd.
ALL	To the shepherd.

They raise their cups to the south and begin to eat. Rose and Miriam remain looking out of the window.

ROSE	Why does the shepherd put bells on his sheep?
MIRIAM	So he can find the ones that go astray.
ROSE	Do many go astray?

MIRIAM One in a hundred? The other ninety-nine tend to stick together.

MARIA Mary Rose, my dear, you may not know that our prophet Isaiah says that we are like sheep. We have all gone astray at one time or another and – well, Miriam will be able to quote the exact scripture.

SALOME All of us, like sheep, have gone astray. We have each turned to our own way. And the Lord has laid on him the iniquities of us all. [56]

MARIA Salome knows the scriptures backwards too, of course.

MADELEINE Like a lost lamb I have wandered away. Search, search for me, your servant, because I have never forgotten your commandments.[57]

MARIA Madeleine was a star student at scripture school, I'm sure. Mary Rose, you know she's a doctor?

ROSE A doctor!

SALOME Of course she's a doctor. Why do you think she talks about her clients all the time?

ROSE Oh, I thought –

MADELEINE You thought what?

ROSE I thought – well, I don't like to say.

SALOME Rose, you can say anything you want here. We're not in a play. We don't have to apply to the authorities for permission to utter what we believe. Within these four walls we can say anything we like. We're not going to be hauled off for profanity and sedition. So speak. Speak.

ROSE It's just that I thought, from something I heard –

Five Marys Waiting: Scene 4 – Evening

MADELEINE   You thought I lived by my wits.

ROSE   Yes, I did.

MADELEINE   Well, you're quite right. I do.

Silence.

MARIA   Like a lost lamb I have wandered away. That's a Psalm of David, isn't it? Mary Rose, I can tell you something about that Psalm. It goes through the alphabet in sections – every verse of each section starts with the next letter on. Very clever.

ROSE   Alpha, beta, gamma, delta?

MARIA   Yes, but in Hebrew of course.

MIRIAM   Alef, bet, gimel, daleth –

ROSE   Epsilon, zeta, eta, theta –

MIRIAM   He, vav, zayin, het –

Enjoying the game, Rose and Miriam race simultaneously through the rest of the respective alphabets to see who finishes first.

ROSE | Iota, kappa, lambda, mu, nu, xi, omicron, pi, rho, sigma, tau, upsilon, phi, chi, psi, omega

MIRIAM | Tet, yod, kaf, lamed, mem, nun, samek, ayin, pe, sadhe, qof, resh, shin, sin, tav

They burst in to breathless laughter as Madeleine and Salome break into spontaneous applause.

MARIA   Sisters, please. Remember Peter. Remember the Lord is watching.

MADELEINE   Maria – and I say this with the utmost love – Peter rests in the Lord's hands. If you have ears to hear, hear these words: If two make peace with each

Five Marys Waiting: Scene 4 – Evening

                    other in this one house, they shall say to the mountain: Be moved!—and it shall be moved.[58] Peter rests safely in the Lord.

SALOME   And anyway, if the Lord is watching, the least we can do is be entertaining.

MADELEINE   Let us make peace, Maria. Let us move the mountain.

Silence.

MARIA   Yes.

                    Yes. A second cup for everyone. Sisters, place your empty cups in front of me side by side. I have a riddle for you.

                    Empty cups now.

They drain their cups and place them as Maria has asked.

                    Now watch. Five empty cups all in a row.

SALOME   Not meant to be us, I hope?

MIRIAM   Who can say?

MARIA   Rose, fill the first three to the brim.

ROSE   Yes, madam.

She fills the first three cups.

MARIA   Now the first three are full. The last two are empty. By moving just one, how can full follow empty, empty follow full?

MADELEINE   Can't be done.

SALOME   I can suggest something useful.

MARIA   What?

Five Marys Waiting: Scene 4 – Evening

SALOME	Pick up the second and drink it dry.
MADELEINE	That doesn't solve it.
SALOME	No, but it would take the edge off your thirst.
MARIA	Salome, you almost got it! I will show you.
	Empty the second into the last and put it back empty.

She does this.

> There! Now full follows empty, empty follows full!

The other women applaud.

ROSE	Full follows empty, empty follows full. Some say that's the secret of the universe.[59]

Silence. The other women look at her curiously.

MIRIAM	The next section. What letter shall it be?
MARIA	B. Every verse to begin with B.
MADELEINE	Blest.
	Blest are the poor in spirit, for theirs is the kingdom of heaven.
SALOME	Blest are those who mourn, for they will be comforted.
MIRIAM	Blest are the meek, for they will inherit the earth.
MARIA	Blest are those who hunger and thirst to do what is right, for they will be filled.
ROSE	Blest are the merciful?
MARIA	Yes.
+ROSE	For they will be shown mercy.

Five Marys Waiting: Scene 4 – Evening

MADELEINE   Blest are the pure in heart, for they will see the Lord.

SALOME   Blest are the peacemakers, for they will be called children of God.

MIRIAM   Blest are you, Salome and Maria and Madeleine and Rose, when people insult you, and persecute you and falsely say all kinds of evil against you because of my son. Be glad and rejoice, because great will be your reward in heaven. For in this same way they persecuted the prophets who were before you.

The distant sound of sheep bells. The repeated cry of a Stone Curlew as it flies over the house. The light is fading into dusk. After a moment, Salome goes to Miriam and kisses her. She looks out of the window.

SALOME   Suppose you had a hundred sheep and you lost just one of them. Would you not leave the ninety-nine grazing in the pasture and search for the lost sheep until you found the one that had gone astray?[60]

MIRIAM   Suppose you had five, and one went astray?

MADELEINE   He loves the music of his flock. The sound of every sheep is different. They may be running away or shaking their heads, and little bells burst out in a sudden clamour or a tinkling cascade, like a stream in the mountain, and all these sounds come together in a kind of harmony.[61]

ROSE   But what use are the bells?

MADELEINE   Why do they have to have a use? They make beautiful music. Does music have a use?

MIRIAM   Rose, do you know the Widow's Lament?

ROSE   What is that?

Five Marys Waiting: Scene 4 – Evening

MIRIAM It's a song. Very popular sometime back. Now you hardly hear it at all.

SALOME I heard a woman singing it this morning on the way to the market. The sun was hardly up but there was something in air. I really thought this might be the day.

MIRIAM You felt that too, Sis?

SALOME I did.

Rose slowly starts humming the song we heard at dawn.

Yes, that's it, Rose.

Don't stop. That's the song.

Rose continues humming as Madeleine speaks.

MADELEINE Song doesn't exist to make us forget about life. It tells us about life. That everything starts and ends. That every note, however beautiful, however odd, connects with the note before, and the note that's coming.

The song is always in danger of disappearing. While it lasts we have to listen, we have to sing. And as we listen, and as we sing, as one note follows another, begins, comes to an end, the song is telling us that everything is connected. That we are alive. And that we will one day die.[62]

Rose stops humming. Silence. In the distance Egyptian and Nubian nightjars have started to call to each other. Again, the distant sound of sheep bells.

MARIA The bells are very useful. Ask any shepherd.

SALOME Do you know any shepherds?

Five Marys Waiting: Scene 4 – Evening

MARIA Yes, Salome, of course I do.

SALOME And of course you've asked them. You've held them in rapt conversation about their bells. I ask this in a very loving way, Maria. I would protect you as I would protect my eye.

MARIA Well, to be truthful, no, Salome, I haven't actually asked them about their bells. But it's obvious, isn't it? The bells will tell them where the flock is or in what direction they are going.

MADELEINE Listen. You can hear them, going from east to west, following the sun.

They listen for a moment.

The bells are the messengers.

MIRIAM I think the shepherd knows better than that. The true shepherd doesn't need the bells to tell him where his flock is or whether the sheep are straying or following the right path. He watches over them. His eyes are good. The bells are his solace. As he cares for his sheep.

SALOME Maybe the sheep like the tinkling too. Just like us. The tinkling of our voices. The jokes. The chatter.

MARIA As we wait.

They listen. Silence.

ROSE Knock, knock!

SALOME Who's there?

ROSE No one.

SALOME No one who?

ROSE No one to watch over me.

Five Marys Waiting: Scene 4 – Evening

SALOME He will. He does.

Silence.

MIRIAM When is a door not a door?

ROSE When it's ajar.

Silence.

ROSE When is a door not a jar?

SALOME When it's closed.

MIRIAM What?

Silence.

MARIA It's easier to open a jar than a door.

Silence. The other women look at her curiously.

MADELEINE When is adore not adore? When we disagree? Let's endure and adore one another – even if we disagree.[63]

Silence.

ROSE Brothers and sisters have I none,

But this man's mother loves his mother's son.

MADELEINE It's the man we've all been talking about.

ROSE Yes. Miriam's firstborn. I may not know much, but this I do know. Miriam loves him.

MARIA As do we all.

SALOME But Rose, he had brothers and sisters.

MARIA *Has* brothers and sisters.

Five Marys Waiting: Scene 4 – Evening

ROSE The first bit is me. Brothers and sisters have I none.

The first bit is me.

Silence.

MIRIAM Dare we light a lamp?

MARIA No! The house must look empty.

ROSE I'm scared.

SALOME Keep talking. Keep your heads down and your voices low, but for God's sake just keep talking.

That way, he'll know we're here.

Absolute silence. Outside it is night. Moonlight has begun to shine in through the east window and it bathes the room in an eerie light.

This is not a play. We don't have to fear what we say. Speak. Speak.

Silence. Maria starts to speak, quietly, brightly, but with increasing difficulty as she seeks to keep a grip on her emotions.

MARIA Who can find a capable wife? Her value is far beyond pearls. Her husband trusts her from his heart. She works to bring him good, not harm, all the days of her life. She procures wool and flax and works with willing hands. She is like those merchant vessels, bringing her food from afar.

It is still dark –

It's still dark when she rises to feed her household and instruct the young women serving her. She gathers her strength and throws herself into her work. Her lamp stays lit at night.

Five Marys Waiting: Scene 4 – Evening

Distant hoot of a Tawny Owl.

> She reaches out to embrace the poor and opens her arms to the needy. Her husband is known at the –
>
> Her husband – is known at the city gates –
>
> Clothed with strength and dignity, she can laugh at the days to come. Her children arise. They make her happy. Her husband too, as he praises her: 'Many women have done wonderful things, but you – you, my dear –
>
> 'You surpass them all!'
>
> Charm can lie, beauty can vanish –
>
> but a woman who fears the Lord – [64]

Silence.

MIRIAM   What is it that everybody does at the same time?

Silence.

MADELEINE   Grows older.

Silence.

SALOME   My husband lived to a good age. He was much older than me but we lived together thirty years before he died. Not long before the end I said, 'Just think. Our wedding day was thirty years ago. We've brought up five children. We've known suffering, and joy. We've had a hard life, but a good one. Thirty years ago you told me that you loved me. And in all those years you haven't said those words since.' Silence. Then he said, 'If I change my mind, I'll let you know.'

Five Marys Waiting: Scene 4 – Evening

Silence. When the women speak their voices are almost whispers.

ROSE Antioch?

SALOME Yes, Rose.

ROSE I want to speak about Antioch.

SALOME Speak.

ROSE It was dusk. A very clear night. There was a bright moon in the sky. Everyone had gone inside to eat. Everyone but me.

My father and mother and my brothers and sisters had just sat down at the table and I had been sent out to get some water from the well. And as I was carrying the jug back to the house I thought I was having a fit, like my sister Junias sometime had, because I was starting to shake and I dropped the jug and it smashed on the ground.

And I looked at our house. And the walls were falling in. And I could hear my parents calling out and the screams of my sisters and my brothers groaning and I shouted NO. And I looked round for help and all the buildings all around were caving in and the screaming was coming from everywhere and seemed to go on and on for ever.

And then it stopped. And there was nothing. No sound. No movement. Nothing.

Just the rubble. The piles of stones all around me.

The moonlight.

Silence.

MIRIAM Like every human being, he was mortal. A son of Adam who was made from soil. My son was conceived in the pleasure of knowing a man. It was the getting of wisdom. For nine months his flesh took shape in the blood of my womb. When he was born, he came into the world like anyone else, began to breathe the same air we all breathe. And like all newborn babies I have ever heard, the first sound he made was a cry. I clothed him and cared for him. He grew. No king ever began life differently.

Was he a king? The wisdom we've been waiting for? A lord for all of us. I don't know. But I do know this. For all of us there is only one way into life, and there is only one way out.[65]

Silence.

MADELEINE For me, he shone so bright and never grew dim. All those who loved him and looked for him always found him. He was quick to make himself known to anyone who was looking. Looking for what's under the skin. Get up early in the morning to search him out, and there he is! He's at your door! You can just invite him in.

It was so easy to fasten your attention on him. He knew you through and through. It's still like that. Even now he's gone. There's this silence. A kind of knowing. He's with me here. Even now. The truth is within.

If you do not know yourselves you live in poverty. If heaven is in the sky then the birds are there already. If it's in the sea, then the fish are there already. You are children of the universe. Heaven is within you and among you. Know yourselves and you will find it.[66]

Five Marys Waiting: Scene 4 – Evening

Silence.

MARIA He brings such perfect peace. He'll come back and find us wherever we are. He will come when you least expect him.[67] Look for him, Rose. He's kind. He'll be with you in every thought. Look for him. He'll be there. Waiting at the door. He's knocking, looking for those who are worthy. Just let him in.

Silence.

MIRIAM Forgive me, Rose. Forgive me, Maria.

The graffiti.

I drew it back again. To solve the riddle.

Silence. The other women look at her curiously.

MADELEINE A square. A triangle. A circle.

ROSE The centre everywhere, the circumference nowhere.[68]

MARIA An upturned cross.

MIRIAM What?

SALOME The fishing boat heaves but never quite sinks.

Silence. Hoot of a Tawny Owl.

At the gate outside, a gentle knocking.

No one moves.

The knocking continues as the light fades.

BLACKOUT

WAITING

David Banks

♩=70

A minor

Mor - ning sings with pro - mise and war - ning. Mid - day whis - pers, 'the ti - me is here'. The long aft - er - noon is wait - ing, wait - ing. Eve - ning des - cends with re - gret and fear. Night is for sor - row and watch - ing for mor - ning. We car - ry the pa - st, be it di - stant or near.

NOTES

[1] Isaiah 31:5a

[2] Isaiah 31:5b

[3] Psalm 84:3-4

[4] Exodus 13:6

[5] Exodus 13:4

[6] A purifying bathing facility that remains in ritual contact with a natural source of water as required by regulations laid down in the Torah.

[7] Acts 5:38

[8] Acts 5:39

[9] Galatians 1:23

[10] Daniel 12:11. This period of about three and half years, that is prophesied between the 'taking away of the daily sacrifice' and the coming of the abomination, has been the subject of much diverse interpretation. Miriam is taking it to mean the death of her son, a sacrifice so great that daily sacrifice is no longer required, and the appearance of Saul as their persecutor or abomination.

[11] Zechariah 13:7 ; Matthew 26:31 ; Barnabas 5:12

[12] Yeshúa first became a known form of the name Yehoshua during the second Temple period (538 BC – 70 AD). Both the full form Yehoshua and the abbreviated form Yeshúa, were in use during the Gospel period – and in relation to the same person, as in the Hebrew Bible references to Yehoshua/Yeshúa son of Nun, and Yehoshua/Yeshúa the high priest in the days of Ezra. It's reasonable to assume that this is what Miriam's son was called by those who knew him.

[13] After Plautus, Roman playwright (c. 254–184 BC)

[14] Merriam-Webster Dictionary defines Pagan as: 'Heathen 1; especially: a follower of a polytheistic religion (as in ancient Rome); 2 one who has little or no religion and who delights in sensual pleasures and material goods, an irreligious or hedonistic person.'

[15] see *Alain Badiou: a life in writing*, an interview with Stuart Jeffries, The Guardian, 18 May 2012

[16] From the Apostles' Prayer (Acts 4:25)

[17] see *Son of Man*, a play by Denis Potter, 1969. The treatment of the subject matter led to Potter being accused of blasphemy by Mary Whitehouse. She later successfully brought a case of blasphemy against James Kirkup for his poem *The Love that Dares to Speak its Name*.

[18] Gospel of Thomas 77

[19] Gospel of Thomas 39

[20] Gospel of Thomas 21

[21] Miriam is right about the return of these birds. But both she and Madeleine are mistaken in calling them swallows. In early spring here is an annual return of the Common Swift *Apus Apus* from South Africa to nest in the Western Wall – one of migrating birds' oldest nesting colonies in the world, according to Professor Yossi Leshem, director of the Israel Ornithological Center for the Study of Bird Migration. 'During mid-February, it arrives in Israel, which is known to be one of its first breeding sites, and migrates back to Africa at the beginning of June, immediately after its nestlings have fledged.' See *The Jerusalem Post*, 'A Swift Return' by Gill Zohar, 3 August 2012.

[22] John 10

[23] According to the four canonical gospels, Joseph of Arimathea was a wealthy man, probably a member of the Sanhedrin, who asked Pilate for the body of Jesus and laid it in his own tomb with, according to Gospel of John, the help of the Pharisee Nicodemus. Both are portrayed as secret disciples of Jesus.

[24] Exodus 22:21

[25] Exodus 13:2

[26] Matthew 6:34

[27] 'from this name the Christ was called a Nazoraean, and in ancient times we, who are now called Christians, were once called Nazarenes', Eusebius, c331. The Gospel of Mark, considered the oldest gospel, consistently uses *Nazarene*

[28] Tao Te Ching, Verse 81

[29] see *The Theologians*, Jorge Luis Borges

[30] Psalms 84:10

[31] after Plautus

[32] see Luke 10:41

[33] see Gospel of Thomas 25

[34] The argument about whether Gentile believers should become Jews (essentially, for males, be circumcised) is not resolved until the Council of Jerusalem in 50 CE when James the Less, or the Just, the brother of Jesus, who has by that time has become leader of the Jerusalem church, makes the apostolic decree that Gentile converts need not be circumcised.

[35] Matthew 10:5-6

[36] John 10:16

[37] Psalms 113

[38] Psalms 114

[39] see Luke 2:36-38

[40] see Mark 10:25, Luke 18:25, Matthew 19:25 and Babylonian Talmud, Baba Mezi'a, 38b. What Salome and Madeleine say is a confusion of both oral traditions.

[41] said to be from the Babylonian Talmud though I haven't been able to locate it.

[42] Luke, 6:44, Matthew 7:16-20; also see James 3:12

[43] Apostles' Prayer (Acts 4:25)

[44] Psalms 16:13

[45] see Gospel of Thomas 102

[46] Matthew 23:27

[47] Matthew 15:13-14, Luke 6:39-40, Gospel of Thomas 34

[48] see Gospel of Thomas 16, Luke 12:49-51, Matthew 10:34

[49] Gospel of Thomas 17

[50] see 1 Thessalonians 5. This letter to the Thessalonians is universally assented to be an authentic letter of Paul and one of the most ancient Christian documents in existence. It is typically dated c. 50/51 CE. My assumption is that these words of encouragement to the persecuted church reflect what he might have been saying and writing since early in his ministry.

[51] Biblical scholarship currently holds that it was several decades after the date of this play that the gospel story began to be written down. Until it was, the story and sayings of Jesus were kept alive and shared among believers by word of mouth. This was not unusual. Many ancient civilisations relied on oral evidence as the main source of historical, mythological and cultural continuity within a society. For example, the Judaic scriptures featuring Solomon were written perhaps three or four hundred years after his death. Formal oral traditions valued accuracy. It is not impossible that a strong and carefully schooled oral tradition could have preserved the details of a story and of significant sayings over centuries. The spoken word may even have been preferable to what was written down. The testimony is embodied in a living person who is trusted – or not. The written word becomes distanced from the living truth. The argument may be that words on the page can be more easily manipulated and serve an agenda which is less easy to discern, whereas the reliability of the spoken word, its accuracy and the testimony of the present teller about their own sources, depends on an immediate sense of the reliability of the speaker.

[52] misquoting Plautus

[53] Plautus

[54] see Genesis 3:15. God speaks to the serpent after the fall of Adam and Eve into sin, 'I will put enmity between you and the woman, between your seed and her seed; He shall crush your head and you shall lie in wait for his heel.' The original Hebrew text and the traditional text of the Septuagint, the Greek Old Testament clearly translate as 'He shall crush your head'. But, for reasons apparently not understood, two ancient translations, the Latin Vulgate (revised by St. Jerome) and the ancient Coptic version (Coptic is the Egyptian language used prior to the Arab Muslim invasions), read, 'She shall crush your head.'

[55] Psalms 23

[56] Isaiah 53:6

[57] Psalms 119:176

[58] Gospel of Thomas 48

[59] Rose may be thinking of the idea at the heart of the I Ching, the ancient Chinese Book of Changes. The full represents Heaven, the empty represents Earth. The dynamic of life emerges in the continuous gradual alternation between these two states. See also the Tao Te Ching, 22:

Yield and overcome
Bend and be straight
Empty and be full
Wear out and be new
Have little and gain
Have much and be confused.

[60] Luke 15:4

[61] See WH Hudson (1841-1922), *A Shepherd's Life*, 11: Starlings and Sheep Bells

[62] See *Guardian* interview with Daniel Barenboim, 25 April 2012

[63] 'Let's adore and endure each other', graffiti painted on a building in Great Eastern Street, London, by street artist Steve 'ESPO' Powers 2012

[64] from Proverbs 31:10-31. Traditionally one of the Sabbath readings on a Friday evening Jewish family gathering.

[65] see The Book of Wisdom 7, one of the seven Sapiential or wisdom books of the Septuagint (Greek Old Testament) – which includes Job, Psalms, Proverbs, Ecclesiastes, Song of Solomon (Song of Songs), and Sirach – and according to St Melito was considered canonical by Jews and Christians in the second century.

[66] Gospel of Thomas 3

[67] see Matthew 24:44, Luke 12:39-40

[68] That the nature of God is a circle or sphere whose centre is everywhere and circumference nowhere is an idea attributed variously to St Augustine, Alain de Lille, Pascal and Voltaire, all of whom postdate the setting of this play. But the origins of the idea may be found in the cosmogenic theory of Empedocles, a pre-Socratic Greek philosopher. Rose may thus be repeating a formulation that was common among well educated Greeks in Antioch.